# JUST A SMALL TOWN GIRL: FREEDOM FROM ABUSE.

Life Story of Amy L. Smith &
How She Became Free From
Sexual Abuse & Alcohol & Drug Abuse,
And The Effects of Abuse.

## Amy L. Smith

Unless otherwise identified, all Scripture quotations are taken from the *King James Version* of the Bible.

Scripture quotations marked AMP are taken from the AMPLIFIED BIBLE, Old Testament Copyright © 1965, 1987 by the Zondervan Corporation. The Amplified New Testament copyright @ 1958, 1987 by The Lockman Foundation. Used by permission.

Scripture quotation marked NIV are taken from the Holy Bible, New International Version®, NIV® Copyright ©1973, 1978, 1984, 2011 by Biblica, Inc.® Used by permission. All rights reserved worldwide.

All scriptures are emphasized by italics.

The stories in this book reflect the author's recollection of events. Some names, locations, and identifying characteristics have been changed to protect the privacy of those depicted. Dialogue has been re-created from memory.

Just A Small Town Girl:-Freedom From Abuse.
Copyright © 2018 Amy L. Smith
All rights reserved!
ISBN-13: 978-1720320869
ISBN-10: 1720320861

*Contact*
Amy L. Smith
P.O. Box 298
Fergus Fall, MN. 56538-0298

Printed in the United States of America. All rights reserved! This book or portions thereof may not be reproduced in any form without prior written permission from the author.

# Foreword

By Zac Smith

I am excited to honor my wife and introduce her book, *"Just A Small Town Girl: Freedom From Abuse."* Today, there are many children, youth, and adults being easily seduced and trapped into sexual abuse, and they don't know how to discern or turn away from toxic relationships.

Amy shares her personal story when she was manipulated into a sexually abusive relationship at the young age of twelve, by a perverted man almost forty years old, which lasted for eight years. Like many today, this sexual control led to alcohol and drug abuse and severe consequences. She shares how she had to deal with these issues, and ultimately, she came to believe in God.

If you love to read drama and trauma stories with a happy ending, you will enjoy reading her detailed life story. She shares her dynamic story how she was abused for many years and got free from the abuse and toxic relationships when she found genuine love that led her in the right direction in life.

She is not ashamed of the gospel of Jesus Christ, for her powerful testimony gives hope to those who felt there was no hope and shows how God can change people who were trapped and stuck in years of abuse and toxic relationships.

# Acknowledgments

First and most of all, I want to thank God for putting it on my heart to write this book and giving me the ability to put my experience into writing. I give Him all the glory on how He turned my mess into a purpose. I want to thank Him for how He loved me and transformed my heart and life and molding me into a new person in Christ.

Secondly, I want to thank my husband and family for loving me so unconditionally and standing by me in my decision to share my story. You all inspire me and remind me to count my blessings every day.

Thirdly, I want to thank my brothers and sisters in Christ and true friends for walking along side me and loving and supporting me in my healing process and loving me even when I wasn't very lovable.

Lastly, I want to thank my Pastor and spiritual leaders for being a lamplight at my feet, directing my path, and building me up to become a better woman and sister in Christ.

And to all those who have graciously supported me to get this book written and published, you are so greatly appreciated!

# Contents

Just A Small Town Girl:
Freedom From Abuse.

Introduction

| | | |
|---|---|---|
| 1 | Danger of Toxic Relationships. | 1 |
| 2 | Recognizing Sexual Abuse. | 11 |
| 3 | Sexual Abuse Creates Coping Mechanisms. | 23 |
| 4 | Toxic Relationships Destroy Self-Esteem. | 37 |
| 5 | Strongholds Are Hard To Cut. | 55 |
| 6 | Too Much Will Make You Try To Escape From Reality. | 79 |
| 7 | God's Foundation Is a Firm Foundation. | 109 |

About The Author

# INTRODUCTION

This true story of the life of Amy L. Smith, *"Just A Small Town Girl: Freedom From Abuse,"* is filled with drama, trauma, and the sorrows and hopelessness of sexual abuse and other abuses and how God set her free.

Amy's story is a very needed book for people to better understand and get people away from toxic deceivers who manipulate and seduce people to steal their will under the false pretense of love.

This life-changing book is valuable to people who are desperate for freedom from a struggle with any kind of abuse or toxic relationships. Her eye-opening story exposes how children, teens, and adults can be easily seduced and trapped into sexual abuse and alcohol and drug abuse and other abuses. She carries a message to help people become free from any kind of abuse.

Amy begins her story with her blissful childhood years on the farm and how her joy changed into sorrow when she was deceived and seduced into a sexual toxic relationship at the age of twelve.

She shows how the married abuser manipulated her will by flattery under the guise of love. Because of his manipulation, he tricked her will into being his secret mistress and had controlled her actions to do what he wanted.

Read how she lost her self-esteem and swore to keep the sexual abuse a secret for years. She shares how she tried to cut ties with the abuser and failed due to confusion and fear created by a compilation of effects stemmed from sexual abuse.

Due to the compilation dynamics to cut ties with her abuser, she tried to escape reality by abusing alcohol, which eventually led to drug abuse. When she became friends with drug addicts and dealers, she fell even lower in isolated despair. It wasn't until Amy came to a dead end and finally became desperate to be free, when her life was changed for the better! She shares how she became totally free from the detrimental effects of sexual abuse, alcohol and drug abuse and toxic relationships and how she experienced God's love that changed her entire life and He turned her sorrow into joy.

# Chapter 1
## Danger of Toxic Relationships.

*"He who walks [as a companion] with wise men will be wise. But the companions of [conceited, dull-witted] fools [are fools themselves and] will experience harm"* (Proverbs 13:20, AMP).

The Bible says if you associate yourself with wise men or women, soon their pure and godly words and lifestyle will influence you to walk in righteousness.

On the contrary, if you associate yourself with a self-confident fool who will not obey God's Word and you are a close friend to him, he will influence you with ungodly and sinful ways and cause you to be a fool and bring you into destruction.

When I was a child, my parents taught me morals and manners. I also had wholesome friendships. However, when I befriended people who weren't raised in a similar manner, I became a follower, instead of a leader. I figured my parents didn't know everything about life and I began to take on a mindset of a fool.

Therefore, things grew worse and worse after my blissful years as a child. I didn't always believe in God. I fell away from my Christian values and quit believing in God. There was a time I didn't believe in much of anything. The outcome was complete self-destruction. I messed up everything in my life with both good and bad intentions.

As a result, it wasn't until I lost everything and had nothing left to lose when I took a leap of faith that brought me to God, and He filled me with joy and contentment like I never had before.

After God transformed my life, He became the center of it all. It was then when I began to associate with wise people of God.

You will read more about this in later chapters, but first, let me begin with my early years, and then you will read how I became acquainted with toxic people who I followed down the road to destruction.

## My Blissful Years
## As A Young Child.

My early years were blissfully simple. As a child I was an inquisitive and busy little green-eyed girl. I was a tomboy and a little farm girl with messy curly light brown hair. My parents would tell you, I was always getting into something. My personality was a trailblazer, but I could be just as sweet and very smart.

There was a big age difference between my dad and mom. My dad, Finn was older than my mom. He was a skinny average height man with dark brown hair and green eyes framed with the big square glasses that were popular in the 80's. He was a hard worker as a mechanic or on the farm with the cows but always made time for us kids.

I liked the way my dad would include us kids with some of his farm chores by giving us rides in the tractor bucket or on the trailers he hauled. Whenever he mowed the lawn, he would take turns giving each of us kids a ride in his lap. He let us help feed the cattle and different things like that.

In those years as a child, I remember my mom, Scarlett. She was a medium sized woman. She had brown curly hair and big brown eyes that were also framed by the same type of big square glasses. My mom worked at a floral store. Then at home, she was always trying to keep traditions going from holidays and birthdays to little hobbies.

Altogether, I had four siblings. My older brother, Sawyer, was older than me, and my sister was younger than me. We all had moments where we got along and fought. I had two older half-brothers, Everett and Asher who were grown and out of the house.

My family and I grew up on a small hobby farm. Our farmstead had a homey inviting feel to it. I always loved driving up the gravel driveway to our house.

We lived in a big white farmhouse with brown trim. There were trees of all kinds and sizes scattered across the farm. My favorites were the apple, pear, and cherry trees. I also loved the grapevines and raspberry bushes. We had a big garden where we would grow fruits and vegetables as well.

The farmstead was on almost ten acres containing a big two-story barn with lots of beef cattle as well as a few other out buildings. We had a black lab dog named Lady and quite a few barn cats.

There was an older lady named Mary who lived on the farm too. She lived in a trailer behind our house. She had lived there when my parents bought the place, and they told her she could stay put. Usually, I would visit her daily, and she would give me a snack of whatever she had baked. We visited for a while, then I continued with my day.

The grass grew green in the summer, and the snow was feet deep in the winter. My siblings and I were always outside playing.

In the summer, we would ride our bikes, build forts in the woods, and explore the farm. In the winter, if we weren't sledding or building snow forts, we were in the barn playing on a rope swing. We would take the rope and climb the hay bales and jump off the bales swinging to the other side of the barn where we would land in a huge mound of soft hay.

Lucky for us kids, we had neighbor kids right across the road who were the same age as us, and we played with them every chance we got. Life was good!

My childhood was happy. I was in sports, 4-H Club, Girl Scouts, and church activities. We had family vacations and spent the summers at my grandparents' lake house, which was fun. We would swim practically all day. I had some of my fondest memories there.

## My Whole Life Changed
## When My Parents Divorced.

I hadn't experienced anything that really rattled my life until I was in the fifth grade. One day, my siblings and I came home from school like usual, but when we walked into the house, it was pretty much empty besides a few boxes and the kitchen table.

My mom and grandparents were there and sat us down at the table. My mom told us she was divorcing my dad.

Then I cried. It was the first time I really felt deeply hurt in my heart. I thought divorce was something you only heard of happening to other people. They tried to talk to us to reassure us that everything will work out, but my whole life just crumbled.

I really hurt for my dad because he was hunting up North. I couldn't stop thinking about how he was going to come home to an empty house. We left the farm the next day and moved into a house in town.

Our new house was a cute little tan stucco house that sat up on a hill. There was an apple tree in the back yard and a weeping willow tree in the front yard that I loved. The house was really close to our school and some of our friends' houses.

My siblings and I also thought it was cool to have cable television. Before that, we only had three channels through an antenna on the farm. I quickly became a big fan of *Nick at Night*. I loved those old shows, especially, *I Love Lucy* and *Happy Days*.

After we moved, the first couple weeks were shaky. We were all adjusting to our new life. I didn't get to see my dad for a month until the courts figured out custody arrangements. It happened to be my birthday when we first saw him after the divorce. My brother, sister, and I got to ride the bus home after school like we use to do before we moved.

It was strange going back to the farm. Since we had left the farm, fall had turned into winter. When we walked into the house we were all quiet while we looked around taking in the changes. There was different furniture that did not match and had scarcely replaced the old furniture, but the necessities were all there.

Later, when I asked my dad where he got the furniture, he explained how family and friends had given him different pieces. I was very grateful they had taken care of him.

That night, to celebrate my birthday we had a pasta dish. I thought it was a white sauced mac-n-cheese, but later realized it was elbow macaroni smothered in milk and butter. I knew my dad didn't have much money after we left. However, it wasn't until years later when I realized how poor he was then, but I watched how hard he worked at getting everything back together.

After supper, all of us went out to the store, and I was excited to pick out a birthday present. It was a three-in-one gift. I could use the gun to play with darts or pellets and use it as a BB gun. We went back to the farmhouse to set up a target area in the basement and took turns shooting the darts until it was time to go home.

Eventually, my life adjusted to the various changes of a divorced family lifestyle. Still, we were active in our after school activities. We still had chores and rules, but the discipline had changed. The consistency wasn't there. My parents tried. Like any single-parent family, there is only a certain amount of attention you can give to your children and continue to work and keep up with the house.

## Danger of Hanging With The Wrong Crowd.

I thought I was living an exciting life when I started to hang with a new crowd. The ironic thing about peer pressure is that it comes from friends and friends of friends, not from complete strangers.

Throughout my young years, I chose to hang with people who I identified as my friends. I wish I would have read the Bible to know its teachings when I was younger. However, I had no idea how serious God's Written Word was for me. I went to church, but I didn't take it seriously.

Hanging with the people of the world was familiar to me, and they were my friends. As a child I thought like a child, and I didn't have the wisdom of an adult. My parents directed my the right way, but I did not listen and went the other way, following my foolish friends down a road that led to destruction.

It is crucial that we are aware of the danger of hanging with people who are not morally grounded, especially as an adolescent, because developmentally, there is a fight for independence and the influences are strong.

This is so important for who we hang with will affect our lifestyles, actions, habits, and desires and will influence us to do evil or do what is right. If we are around wrong influence, then we will follow them without realizing the danger of the wrong influence.

Also, I wish I would have understood the benefits of obeying God's Word to keep me out of the hell I suffered for many years. Church was not a regular, consistent part of my life, even though my parents tried to encourage me to attend church. Consequently, I had never felt the wonderful love of Jesus or had that firm foundation to stand on.

The Bible principles are our tools and road map to prepare us for Heaven, our eternal home after we die. Living out the pirnciples of the Bible allows us to live a victorious and joyful life in Christ while we are here on earth.

Daily, we are faced with a spiritual battle of good and evil, no matter what our age. If we are raised on a firm foundation that's filled with God's healthy love, attention, support, and encouragement, we are built stronger to defend ourselves from evil influences.

However, there are many generations of broken people raising broken people because they don't know how to break the cycle and become healthy people who are spiritually, mentally, emotionally, and physically sound.

Furthermore, these broken people influence other people in their broken way, and peer influence wins, which boils down to evil wins and Satan wins.

The only way we can beat the devil is to know and live out the God breathed words of the Bible. Live the principles until they become habit, and the habit becomes your way of life.

I stress this so vehemently because I was spiritually blinded to the truth, and I got snagged up as a slave to the devil for many years. As you will read in this book, I will share how I fell into the awful hell traps of sexual abuse, alcohol abuse, and drug abuse and went to prison.

Despite all the hell I went through the next years of my life, I can tell you that the hand of God was on me and kept me from dying and going to hell.

I am thankful that God knows all things, and there is nothing hidden from Him. He knows everything, and He knew that the day would come when I would write my testimony in this book about the sorrows of the abuse and toxic relationships I suffered when I walked in darkness. He knew I would tell the good news how Jesus set me free, restored me, and transformed my life to serve Him, and it would affect many lives and set them free.

As I stated previously, I did not realize the destruction that waited ahead of me while I was walking with lost, unrooted people. I just wanted friends to have fun with them. Typical of children and youth today, I was influenced by my peers. I wanted to be loved, accepted, needed, and appreciated by my peers.

If children and young people don't feel loved or accepted due to deep hidden hurts, they lose their self-esteem and seek to be accepted by their peers. Children will look to be loved by someone else or others when they don't feel loved, appreciated, or needed. That is what happened to me.

Let me continue with my story. When I was young, I hung with some lost, unrooted friends, and I didn't even know they were lost. I was seeking to feel loved and appreciated by them. I was naïve and innocent and had no idea how they would influence me to be like them.

## Chapter 1. Danger of Toxic Relationships.

I met a new girl named Jade, when my sixth grade year started. She had just moved here with her family from out-of-state. Her mom, Chloe decided to move back closer to where her dad, Lincoln, grew up. Jade had a sister, Layla, who was a little older but in the same grade as us, and she had a brother, Jackson, who was older than her.

It didn't take long for Jade and me to be friends. We became friends pretty much immediately.

She was different than the other girls in the school where I went. She was cute with blue eyes and blond shoulder length hair. She wore makeup with skater clothes but was super nice and outgoing. We had every class, lunch, and recess together.

Shortly after we became friends, I was invited to her house after school. She was living in a townhouse apartment until her parents found a house to buy, which was about four blocks away from where I lived.

We sat outside on the front door cement steps while we enjoyed talking and drawing designs and little sayings on her legs with lipstick.

It was a beautiful end of summer day. It was warm without the humidity and the kind of day that can give a person nostalgia.

After a while, her dad, Lincoln pulled up in his fancy car. I could tell he favored his car by how clean and shiny he kept it. Lincoln was a distinguished athletic guy with blondish grey hair and green eyes.

Lincoln got out of his car and walked past us, and shouted at Jade saying, "Jade, go change and wash off your legs! You look like a slut!" Then he walked into the house.

I was completely stunned. Instantly, I had a bad impression of Lincoln, and I could not believe he would speak so degrading to his own daughter.

Jade's mood had changed instantly, and she told me that her father was a bad guy, describing him with a "not-so-nice" word. I tried to defend her and tell her that she didn't look bad, but I don't think she believed me. I went home shortly after that.

As the days and weeks went by, the friendship between Jade and I continued to grow stronger. We would do everything together.

On the weekends, my dad would usually bring us to the roller-skating rink. We would have sleepovers, do our hair and make-up, and dress-up. We listened to all kinds of music and choreographed dances.

Eventually, I also became friends with Jade's sister, Layla. We didn't hang out as much at first because she hung out with an older crowd that smoked, drank, and did drugs. Jade wasn't doing any of that yet.

However, the influence didn't take long to embrace me. One day while walking home from school, I chose to start hanging out with Layla along with another friend of ours.

On the way home, Layla stopped to smoke a cigarette and offered us one. That was when I tried my first cigarette. It was so disgusting, but it made me feel like I was cool and older. So, from then on, I would "smoke" but not inhale.

Hanging with these new friends had opened me to a whole new world in my life. They were teaching me new things like new lingo, music, and boys.

What was even more exciting was the housing decision of Jade and Layla's parents. They bought a house that was a few houses from my mom's house. Jade and I could practically see each other from our bedroom windows.

After that, my world changed the first time I stayed overnight at the home of Jade and Layla. The atmosphere was totally different. Their parents were so different and relaxed on their parenting styles. My parents seemed so strict, compared to them. There wasn't really any rules to follow at Jade's and Layla's home.

That night a group of us played the game, *Truth or dare spin the bottle*. We played for quite a while until Jackson, Jade's and Layla's brother, was dared to kiss me for five minutes. It was my first kiss ever and we just never stopped. Everyone went to bed and we were still kissing. We would fall asleep for a little while, then wake back up and start kissing again.

Because of not sleeping enough, I was extremely tired the next morning. I had to get up early because my dad came to get me for church. I could just about imagine how I looked. My eyes felt like sandpaper. All I wanted to do was go home and get more sleep.

I continued to follow the influences of my new friend. Eventually, Layla introduced me into trying alcohol and weed with her. I didn't care for weed, and I didn't smoke it for a while after I tried it, but I continued to drink. Jade also started to smoke and drink with us, too, but didn't smoke pot.

Jade's and Layla's dad, Lincoln, and his brother, Jasper, would give alcohol to us girls when they would come home from fishing.

We would usually get to drink beer. It was either Pucker or Mudslide. I didn't drink much, but I would just take a few sips because I didn't like the feeling of being buzzed.

The destruction of my life did not stop there, but only grew worse.

# CHAPTER 2
## Recognizing Sexual Abuse.

*"Every tree that does not bear fruit is cut down and thrown into the fire. Thus, by their fruit you will recognize them"* (Matthew 7:10, NIV).

One of the number one ways an abuser or adulterer approaches a child or woman, is by lustful words of flattery to entice her and lure her into his arms. He wakes up her emotions by telling her that he loves her and she is very beautiful and special to him, and he kisses her. Soon, he gets her trapped to steal her emotions under the guise of making her feel loved. That is how he begins to make her a victim of sexual abuse. The professional label to this kind of behavior is called "Grooming."

Grooming is the process an abuser uses to sexually abuse a person. An abuser will target his victim, build trust, and create some sort of comforting connection. Then, an abuser will look for ways to get their victim alone to sexually abuse them. Afterwards, to control his victim's secrecy and will, he will blame the victim, instill fear, create doubt and guilt, or some kind of dependency for the victim so the victim remains silent and positional for continual abuse.

Sexual abuse is any kind of sexual misconduct with a child. It can exposing an abuser to a minor, fondling of a victim or abuser, masturbation, photos taken of a child or abuser sent to a child, sexual intercourse (vaginal, anal, or oral), and sex trafficking of a child, woman, or man.

I did not know Lincoln as a sexual abuser then. Much later in life, I came to realize that he was an abuser and a pervert and liar.

Lincoln disguised himself as my friend, but in reality, he was my enemy. The Bible says it this way, *"Faithful are the wounds of a friend [who corrects out of love and concern], But the kisses of an enemy are deceitful [because they serve his hidden agenda]"* (Proverbs 27:6, AMP).

There can be toxic relationships without sexual abuse, as well. Adulterers, narcissism, liars, co-dependency, jealous or control freaks, and other type of abusers, such as physical, emotional, verbal and psychological abusers, makes for toxic relationships. With any one of them, the outcome is usually devasting, unless the toxic person has an extreme change in his lifestyle to make him into a healthy person. However, I need to add that this sort of change does not take place overnight.

In this chapter, I will share how I became a victim of sexual abuse that began at twelve years old, by being molested by an abuser who was around forty years of age. This led to losing my virginity by his conniving sexual encounters. The abuse led to further entrapment and the deception of a sickening toxic relationship that lasted for years.

I lost my self-esteem and will by being violated in my young years, which started a cycle of repeated years of sexual abuse and other abuse. I also developed coping mechanisms that took me years to let go of them after surrendering my will to God, hours of counseling and therapy sessions, as well as just striving to live a healthier life.

Therefore, I will not share my story to glorify the devil and his works, but my purpose is to glorify God by helping people understand sexual abuse and toxic relationships and tell people how God changed my life completely as shared in later chapters.

**Violated.**

Let me continue from the previous chapter when hanging out with Jade. It was in the beginning of February when I was sitting at Jade's house, and we were the only ones home until Jade's mom, Chloe, came home. She was rail thin with dark olive colored skin and dark eyes. Chloe worked the night shift at a café.

It was obvious she was angry when she walked in the house. Jade immediately asked what was wrong. Chloe explained how she got off work and Lincoln never came to pick her up, so she walked home in the cold. Then, Chloe went on to share her suspicions that Lincoln was having an affair with their friend, Nora, who was also the mom of Jackson's girlfriend.

However, just as that conversation started, Lincoln walked in drunk and reeked with beer. He walked directly to Chloe and started kissing on her and was trying to make an overzealous effort at apologizing. When that wasn't really working, he suggested he order pizza for everybody.

After the pizza was ordered, Lincoln took notice of how Jade was acting standoffish towards him, too. To get Jade laughing, he started wrestling with her, putting her in different holds and tickling her. When he put her in a hold she couldn't get out of, Jade yelled for me to help her, so I jumped in to get him to let her go.

Once I jumped into their brawl, Lincoln's attention immediately shifted to me, and he started flipping me around to have me face a wall. I felt his hand slide across my breast. I was completely thrown off at this point and began to question if that was sexual or not. Then, it happened again, and that uncomfortable feeling began to accompany my mind, full of questions.

The wrestling stopped shortly after that, and Jade and I went upstairs to her bedroom. I pretty much blurted out what happened when we got upstairs, but Jade told me that she thought it was just an accident, and she didn't think her dad would ever do something like that on purpose.

Reluctantly, I skeptically believed her because I wanted to think he did not do it intentionally. Yet, I went home with a mind full of doubts and the lingering feeling of his hand still sliding across my breast.

Soon, I knew it was true and was not my imagination. In the days that followed, he had groped me a few other times while trying to wrestle with Jade and me. I tried to ignore it at first, and when he continued I began to fight him harder. I didn't say anything because I found it really embarrassing. This is how a child abuser defiles a child by slowly introducing her to the grooming acts and deceiving her will before she is mature and of age.

Then one evening, Jade and Layla called me to come over to their house. They went shopping all day with Nora and wanted to show me their new clothes.

After I arrived and saw their clothes, Jade and Layla went out to the garage to hang out with Lincoln and Nora. They were drinking beer and visiting. Lincoln started wrestling with Jade and Nora. I mainly just sat and watched with Layla until she rose up and left, and then I would help Jade from time-to-time.

While they wrestled, I saw Lincoln grab on Nora in the same way he would do to me, but I also noticed that she laughed and didn't seem to mind. It pretty much confirmed everyone's suspicions that there was an affair happening between them, but I didn't say a thing about it to anybody.

Then for whatever reason, Nora and Jade left and walked into the house saying they will be right back. That left me alone with Lincoln. I was uncomfortable sitting alone with Lincoln in the garage. I tried not to pay attention to him, but immediately he came over to me and started messing with me.

In a few quick movements, he had pulled me off the steps, put me in an arm lock bearhug and walked me over to the corner of the garage.

Lincoln had me face him with my back up against the wall, which was by the garage door. Then, he started to rub my breasts. He asked me if it bothered me when he did that, and I told him it did. He told me he would stop touching me.

Assuming that he meant what he said, I went to walk away, but then he stopped me. He started telling me how he thought I was very beautiful, and he wouldn't ever do anything to hurt me.

In a seductive encouraging voice, he was trying to persuade me that I was special to him and made an excuse for what he was doing to me. He said, "I know that what I am doing is wrong and people won't understand, but this is different."

The sexual abuse was just beginning. My parents warned me about child abusers, but I had this misconception they would look like dirty, creepy people, not fathers of your best friend. As a child, I was extremely vulnerable to his cunning tactics. Lincoln was able to work me over like butter in his hands.

With his smooth voice of manipulation, he told me, "It would cause a lot of trouble between our families if anyone ever found out what I am doing, so don't ever tell it." Insisting that I keep it a hidden secret was another trick to get me in fear and under his control, and that is why I bottled it up inside of me.

In response to keep it secret, I promised I wouldn't say anything because of fear, shame, and embarrassment. Then, he finally let me walk away.

Eventually, I went home and I was feeling very strange. As an innocent minor I felt violated, but I also felt good about myself. I had never been told that I was beautiful like that, and it felt good to hear that I was wanted and someone cared for me. I fell for his trick under the guise of "love" and had no idea that this was a trap from Satan to destroy my life thereafter.

What a trick that child molesters do to play on a child's emotions and manipulate that child! At that early age, I actually thought the man loved me. However, I later learned that sexual abusers choose children because they are ignorant, gullible and naïve.

Meanwhile, the whole situation left me feeling an overwhelming sense of confusion. I debated on saying something to others, but I wasn't sure what would happen if I did. For that reason, I didn't tell anyone about it. I also found it extremely embarrassing to talk about it. After that, I wanted to stay away from him, but at the same time I didn't want to miss out on being with my friends.

Besides that, I believed him when he said he wouldn't hurt me. I just didn't know how to get over the uncomfortable feeling of what was happening.

### My Innocents Was Stolen.

My story is a typical example of how a person becomes deceived by a molester and gets hooked and stuck in a sexual toxic relationship as a child, teenager, or adult.

Here is how it happened to me. I continued to go to Jade's and Layla's home when invited. I trusted myself that I could and would protect myself from whatever it was that was happening to me. However, I soon found out that I could not actually protect myself from harm.

When Lincoln would be at the house, he would start wrestling matches and he continued to grab on me. He even started to grab my crotch and butt. Whenever the groping and fondling occurred, it became an unspoken challenge that I would seriously try to hurt him.

Some of my methods were taking Lincoln's hands and grinding them down the popcorn walls. I gouged at his eyes. I kicked him in the nuts. I even broke one of his fingers.

Sometimes, Lincoln would get so mad at me for the pain I would inflict on him, he would put me in choke holds or sit on my back and push down on my lungs. He would do this until I would almost pass out. He seemed to enjoy inflicting pain, but I refused to shed tears and only fought back harder.

Other times, he would put me in a scissor leg lock and push down with his legs and have my arms in a lock where he would pull up. It felt like he was tearing my body apart. It was probably the most excruciating pain I ever felt before child birth.

When I couldn't get him back, I would spit on him or his car. His car was his baby and he would get mad if people touched it, so when I spit on it or wrote cuss names in the dust on it, he would get furious.

One day, Lincoln suddenly kissed me while I was at their house when I came for the purpose to hang out upstairs with the girls in their room. When I went downstairs to use the bathroom, Lincoln was sitting on the couch. He was by himself while watching the movie, *One Flew over the Coo Coo's Nest*. When he saw me, he insisted for me to come sit by him for a minute.

Then I sat down, and he leaned over and kissed me. The kiss was a shock. I was stunned and speechless. I didn't know what to think. After that, he grabbed my face and told me I was beautiful. I felt so uncomfortable but also elated to be called beautiful again.

That was so strange to me that I ended up going to church the next day, and I told my friend, Delilah about it. For some reason, I couldn't hold it in this time. Then I told my friend, Adelyn as well.

Telling it had backfired on me because Adelyn went back and told Jade and Layla who later confronted me about it. One day in their bedroom, the girls asked me about it. They were wondering if it was true what Adelyn told them. I denied it. They said they needed to tell their folks what she was saying. So, we all ended up going downstairs where Lincoln and Chloe were, and the girls told them what Adelyn said.

Because Lincoln was hearing it, I was scared. I knew I broke my promise in a way. I didn't know what was going to happen. I had seen the immediate surprise on Lincoln's face when he heard what they had to say.

Then he played it off in a joke. With a soft, giddy, and persuasive tone of voice he muttered, "Now, come on over. Aim for your kiss!" and he made a kissy face.

Then with a firm warning, Chloe replied, "Stop hanging around Adelyn if she is going to start stirring up trouble like that." She also exclaimed, "The wrestling needs to stop, too!"

When Chloe said that, I was relieved that it blew over so quickly. However, there was still another look in Lincoln's eyes that was questionable fear or anger. I wasn't sure. I wanted to talk to him, but I didn't know what to say.

Later when I finally had an opportunity to talk to him, out of fear I made up a lie of how Adelyn got things mixed up. The lie was pathetic, and we both knew I had told part of the secret. All he said was, "Don't worry about it."

## Connived Into Intercourse.

Before I continue with my story, let me remind you that the devil preys on broken people to become abusers and break more people. Manipulation is by far the biggest weapon to pressure you and trick you to do whatever he wants and gives you no free choice of your own will to make your own decisions in life.

That is the how Lincoln acted. He wore this persona that he cared about me and wanted me happy, and because I was a twelve year old girl, I believed in him and didn't see the ulterior motives. However, I now believe that the only goal he had in mind was to control and use me to please his own lust and sexual gratification.

In a short time, I became a slave to his sexual will. Not aware of it at that time, this is what happens to people who are victimized by an abuser, and they are manipulated in developing toxic sexual relationships.

In simple terms, Lincoln was a pervert who saw nothing wrong with his actions. He ruled by a manipulating force of respect and kindness, but sought to dominate me however he wanted and whenever he wanted.

When hanging out with him, I was even more confused and thinking I could protect myself. However, he was conniving with me, and I found out that I could not protect myself.

Besides that, he had a wife, but according to his perverted thinking, she was not enough for him. She was just another pawn in his game of chess used only when he felt necessary.

As I stated before, I was gullible, vulnerable, and ignorant of the devices and tricks that the devil used to get me trapped. Because I did not know Jesus and never understood how to accept Him in my heart, I was in darkness. Actually, I was spiritually blinded to all of this, and I just wanted to feel loved and accepted.

Now, let me continue with my story. Lincoln acted like he loved me when I was around him, and at the same time, I felt intimidated by his dominance and sexual advances. However, he continued to slowly progress in his advances towards me and he kept working me over to get me comfortable with him.

One evening, after I had supper at my house, the girls invited me to come over. When I got there, Lincoln answered the door and the girls were upstairs. He grabbed me and just started kissing me. All of a sudden, he grabbed my hand and put it on his privates. I froze and didn't move. I felt extremely grossed out.

When I didn't move, he tried teaching me what to do. I felt so humiliated. After that, he started to push my head down towards his private parts. I wasn't sure what he was trying to get me to do. However, I reached a point where I couldn't take any more, and I resisted him, shaking my head no.

I think he could tell that I was scared once he looked at my face. He ended up kissing me some more. Then, he tried to butter me back up with kind words, compliments, and promises. It was nothing but manipulation to keep me under his sexual control.

Over weeks of this happening, I became more confused and did not know how to feel. There were times when we were alone, he would tell me many nice things that he thought of me. His flattery made me feel good and elevated. It puffed me up and allowed me to feel good about myself. After that, groping happened so often that it started to feel normal.

I knew what Lincoln was doing was wrong in a general sense, but he kept telling me how people wouldn't understand and that this was different. Lincoln's kind words would silence the alarms that the wrongness of the situation was setting off.

Let me stop here for a moment and tell you that this is exactly how the devil persuades people to sin. He gives you a taste of evil, and he uses people to try to appeal to your emotions to make it appear that doing wrong is right and it feels good. However, the devil will never tell you that what you are doing will destroy your will and life.

Now, let me go back to sharing my story. Lincoln started asking me if I would let him make love to me one day. I didn't know how to say no because I was intimidated by him. Out of fear I agreed. However, I really was not willing and it was not my will to go through with it. During this situation, it was something about the eggshells I was walking on, and I was too afraid to say no.

One of the next times, I ended up staying the night. As soon as Lincoln found out and got a chance to talk to me alone, he told me he wanted me to sleep on the couch. I questioned myself what to do and debated on going home, but I didn't. Again, I just thought I would be able to handle whatever came at me, but I was deceived.

That night, after we all fell asleep, Chloe went to work the night shift, and Lincoln came out to the living room and woke me. He took my hand pulling me off the couch. Once I was up, he stuffed the blanket I was using with pillows. He did this to make it look like I was still laying there. My heart was pounding as Lincoln brought me back to the computer room where there was a spare bed, and he took my virginity. I was just twelve years old.

After he finished, we went back to the living room where he lit us each a cigarette. He tried to make small talk, but I didn't say anything, and just let my cigarette burn out.

The next day, I went to school not feeling like myself. I felt like I was walking in a daze but continued to act like nothing ever happened.

At that point, my thoughts towards Lincoln were still just as confused as when it all first began. I couldn't quite connect the dots. As far as what he did to me, I felt an emotional disconnection, but I had thoughts I had no clue to get answered. I wondered if I could get pregnant. I questioned myself. I wondered if I was damaged because I was so sore. I kept it quiet and wondered if I should I tell somebody about it. However, I said nothing and didn't trust telling anyone.

The next time when I saw Lincoln, he seemed unusually happy to see me. In a sigh of relief he exclaimed, "I was so scared after that night. I thought you were going to say something, and I kept waiting for the police to show up for me at work!" To make me more confused, he kissed me, and he told me how he cared about me and wouldn't ever do anything to hurt me.

In the weeks that followed, Lincoln pursued two more sexual encounters. Both times he brought me downstairs to the basement and laid me down on an old dirty rug. It happened to be early morning with daylight, and I felt so uncomfortable and embarrassed that he could see my naked body.

The relationship at this point was only about sex. I hardly ever spoke to him but simple answers consisting of yes or no or maybe a sentence. He didn't know anything about me really.

As I recap how this abuse took place, let me make a comment concerning the difference between the plan of God and the plan of the devil in this situation. Obviously, it was not God, but it was the plan of the devil who used Lincoln to steal my virginity at that young age. It wasn't until many years later when I became a Christian and read the Bible about Jesus and His purpose. It was then when I discovered that He gives us abundant life, overflowing with great joy that honors the Lord. If I would have known Jesus then, I would not have gone down the road of continual abuse and destruction.

In the Bible, Jesus clearly described the nature of the devil as a thief whose goal is to rob, cheat, and destroy us, and the nature of Jesus is the opposite, for He gives us life. The Scripture says it this way, *"The thief comes only in order to steal and kill and destroy. I came that they may have and enjoy life, and have it in abundance [to the full, till it overflows]"* (John 10:10, AMP).

The first part of the scripture, which describes the nature of the devil, is an excellent definition of Lincoln and how he was used by the devil to control and destroy my will and life and cheat me of my childhood. From my experience, I can tell you several main ways an abuser controls the will of a child, teenager, or adult. He controls by manipulation, condemnation, and intimidation that steals your freewill.

Contrary to this, the love of Jesus Christ gives you a freewill to accept Him in your heart and life, and He will never force you to do anything. He will give you joy and peace that you never had before, and He will build your confidence and self-esteem. He will never steal your joy, peace, and self-esteem!

Because of those sexual encounters, it messed up my life and brought me into more problems and destruction as you will read in the next chapter.

# CHAPTER 3
## SEXUAL ABUSE CREATES COPING MECHANISMS.

*"He that covereth his sins shall not prosper: but whoso confesseth and forsaketh them shall have mercy"* (Proverbs 28:13, KJV).

Sexual abuse can create many unhealthy side effects to the victims. Many times, victims learn to cope in many different ways without always conscientiously realizing the sexual abuse has driven them this way. Lying, alcohol and drug abuse, sexual addictions, anxiety, depression, feelings of worthlessness, body modifications, eating disorders, OCD, constantly feeling dirty, as well as many other disorders can develop out of being sexually abused.

Occasionally, victims get proper treatment and are resilient enough to bounce back from the abuse. There are healthy coping mechanisms to deal with sexual abuse, as well. Some coping skills include: Biblical practices, talking to your pastor, professional therapy, talking with a close friend, writing, art, music, becoming an advocate, sports and others.

When children, teenagers, and adults hide their sexual abuse and keep the toxic relationship secretly bottled up, they will start using coping mechanisms. I started depending on smoking and alcohol to get rid of the pain. However, none of those negative coping mechanisms ever helps, but only makes matters worse. This is what happened to me, and I had no idea how these abuses would lead me into more and more trouble and pain.

**Moved Away and Missed Home.**

Here is how matters grew worse for me. That spring, a couple months after the beginning of the sexual encounters with Lincoln, I ended up moving a few hours away to a different city so I could live with my mom, my sister, and my mom's boyfriend, Devin. He was a nice guy who lived in a quiet little neighborhood where there were kids my age.

Around the same time my brother, Sawyer, was sent away for his first time to treatment. He spent the rest of his childhood in and out of treatments and juvenile detentions. He was home every so often only to be sent away again for drugs or violence.

When I moved there, I felt lost. I missed my friends and school, and most of all, I missed my dad. Constantly, I would call back home. I usually called and talked to Jade and Layla and occasionally, I talked to Lincoln. Also, I talked to my dad and some other friends.

The first time my mom and Devin got the phone bill, they were furious. There were many hours of long distance phone calls that I had made. The phone bill was over four hundred dollars. Nevertheless, it didn't stop me from calling. After that, every month the phone bill was the same and so were the arguments.

It was in that city when I finished my sixth grade year. It gave me just enough time to meet some new friends. I didn't really like the school because it was too big. My mom also started me in a church program, but I hated to go and would refuse to attend church. As a result, my mom and I would constantly argue over this matter, but I didn't care and stubbornly was determined that I would not go.

Emotionally I felt lost. I had some type of anxiety and I couldn't explain what I was going through. Constantly, I smoked and only felt better when I would go back to my dad's home for a visit. My dad still got us kids every other weekend. I loved going home just for the familiarity.

After I had moved to the city, Lincoln had befriended my dad. Somehow, it came about where Lincoln and Chloe offered to stand up on my dad's behalf for getting custody of us kids.

Sometimes, when I would call Jade, my dad would be over there visiting, and I started to think that Lincoln wasn't such a bad guy after all because my dad liked him.

Before I would come back to visit my dad on the weekend, I started to ask Lincoln to buy his girls and me alcohol so we could drink. It worked out perfectly to party because my dad knew we missed our friends, so he allowed us to have one sleepover a weekend with them, and then the rest of the time was spent with him.

On those weekends, Chloe still worked the night shift as a waitress. So, if the mess was cleaned up by morning, she didn't know about us drinking. Usually on the weekends, the girls and I would drink with Lincoln on Friday nights.

While we drank, we would listen to music, play cards, and visit late into the night. Once when we all passed out, Lincoln would wake me and brought me to his bedroom. At that point since I got to drink, I didn't really care what he did with me. Hanging out with him in this way allowed me to start liking him.

Back in the city, Devin's daughter, Shiloh, came to live with us for the summer. She was sixteen years old and smoked cigarettes, smoked pot, and drank. She was a spoiled brat and the only child and was used to getting her way a lot. It was frustrating sometimes, but most of the time we got along.

Shiloh and I created lots of mischief and caused many fights between our parents because they wouldn't know what to do with us. We snuck out of the house, smoked pot, drank, and smoked cigarettes. Shiloh ended up going back to live with her mother after maybe two months because it was too much for our parents.

### The False Security of Rebellion.

Let me stop my story for a moment to comment about the cause of rebellion. Children and teens can be easily tricked into a deceitfully toxic relationship with a rebellious controlling person. An abused person will eventually fight back in society by rebellion. The more teenagers or adults are sexually abused, the more they rebel and abuse themselves with smoking, alcohol, and/or drugs, which can lead to doing crimes. When an abused person is in rebellion against authority, it gives a sense of false security that makes one think he is stronger and more independent.

Rebellion is deception that controls the will and does not come from God, but from the devil. When teenagers or adults think they are stronger and more independent by rebellion, it is a lie from hell and a sense of false security that results in destruction.

## Chapter 3. Sexual Abuse
### Creates Coping Mechanisms.

The emotion of false security is nothing but a cover-up lie from the devil that makes one think if he uses alcohol and drugs, it will cause him to feel good with a sense of escape from reality. The truth is that rebellion is the nature of the devil, which deceives one to thing he is doing right when actually he is doing wrong.

Let me continue with my story of rebellion. One day, when I was back to my hometown for a visit that summer, I got my first inkling about what I was to Lincoln after the county fair. Jade and I went to the fair when it was in town. We ended up running into two guys who were a few years older than us. We talked to them for a while, and then we all planned on going to the demo derby together.

The next day, the guy named Liam, ended up asking me to be his girlfriend and I accepted, and Jade started to date the other guy named Noah.

I thought Liam was so cool because he had a car and we drove around the next afternoon. We ended up hanging out over at Jade's the next day, and Liam and I had kissed up in Jade's bedroom.

Lincoln was gone doing something at the time and I ended up leaving before he got home, so he didn't see any of it, even though I wasn't trying to hide it. Jade ended up telling him about our weekend at the fair and the boys we met and me kissing Liam in her room.

The next time I saw Lincoln, he was extremely angry! He ignored me at first. Then, he started making fun of me. I was really confused why he was acting like that, but when we were alone, he came out and asked me about Liam. I told him about it, and he just said that he was upset by it because he thought we were a thing.

I wasn't completely sure what he meant by a thing, but I knew he meant our situation was more serious to him than I thought. I had many questions concerning what I was to him because he had a wife and Nora. So, I wasn't his only girl. However, as usual, I asked no questions.

After that, a lady from the county courts ended up coming to interview us kids during my parents' custody battle for sole custody.

She asked us all sorts of questions, and I told her I wanted to live in my hometown with my dad. To make sure it happened, I lied and exaggerated my mom's partying habits and said that I had seen Devin smoking pot. I even told the judge the same thing. I knew I would later regret it, but I didn't want to live in the city and I couldn't tell my mom that without her getting hurt or mad.

Shortly after that, my mom lost the custody battle, and she was crushed. I felt like the worst person ever to see her cry like that. I felt so ashamed. She just asked me why I would say such things. I didn't have a clear answer. I knew that I didn't want to live in the city and tried to reassure her I loved her, but I had never seen my mom look so broken.

It really hurt our relationship. We usually only saw each other a few times a year after that, for a very long time. That decision was not her wish, but it was mine. I just couldn't stand to see her after I lied about her.

The day we found out my dad had won custody, it happened to be a Friday and his weekend to have us. So, my sister and I packed all our bags and left the city to start living back in my hometown within hours of hearing the court's decision.

Living back in our small town was good. I went back into my old school and had no problem adjusting to it. My dad did his best to give my sister and me structure and rules.

We would have supper every night at a certain time and go to church on Sundays. He allowed us to have one sleepover per week. We also had a curfew. Everything went well at first, but I began to push the limits.

I started misbehaving at school. I was constantly getting written up for being disruptive and tardy, and I was involved in some fighting incidents and skipping school a few times. It was something about the negative attention and being rebellious that made me feel stronger and more independent than I actually was.

## Chapter 3. Sexual Abuse
## Creates Coping Mechanisms.

My punishments varied per write up. Most of the time I got detention, but I hated going on my own time after school, so I would usually skip detention. When I skipped it many times, I was given a I.S.S. (IN School Suspension). Then, I would only have to spend a day in trouble on their time. In addition to that, I would get all my late homework done.

I thought I.S.S. wasn't that bad. Actually, the actual room was the worst part about it because it was cold. It was a small room tucked in the downstairs, which was the back of the school that only had a desk for the teacher and a desk for about ten students.

Therefore, my dad would sometimes ground me at home depending on the severity of the trouble. Most of the time, he would sit me down and try to talk to me and get me set back on the right track. I would listen to him and my intentions usually wanted to do better, but it didn't happen. I wasn't willing to change my bad habits of rebellion, and it became worse with over one-hundred and twenty write ups that year while in the seventh grade.

Besides that, there were a few times my dad, the Assistant Principal, and I had a meeting to get me back on the right track, and I would mean-well, but failed. My dad had me see a counselor at a Mental Health center, but Lincoln told me everything I needed to say for the doctor to find no problems in me.

Most of all, my free time was spent at the house of Jade and Layla. We all preferred to be over there because we got to smoke and drink.

We mostly drank on the weekends, but we also drank on some school nights. My dad's rule of only having one sleepover per weekend didn't stay for too long. I usually could get one more during the week when Lincoln would tell me what to say, or he would sometimes talk to my dad for me.

### Lincoln Used Me As His Mistress.

After Lincoln's continual sexual advances, I became his puppet mistress when I was in the seventh grade. Eventually, I fell for Lincoln and my feelings for him were endless. I adored him without knowing any better.

He made me feel I was loved and appreciated when he did sweet things to me that let me know he cared. He started telling me he loved me. He would do little things that showed me he cared and would flirt with me when nobody was looking. Sometimes, he would wink at me or stick out his tongue and crinkle his nose at me.

Other times, he would grab on me, kiss me or hug me when nobody was around. If they were around, he would quickly do it when nobody was looking. Sometimes, he would lure me into the riskiest situations where somebody could have opened a door or turned a head, and we could have been busted fooling around.

Most of his sexual advances manifested when he gave me a ride home at night or when I stayed the night after everyone went to bed. I believed Lincoln loved me, but I associated most of his love with the sexual advances he made because that's all he did to show me affection.

He couldn't take me on dates. I couldn't talk to friends about him. We were stuck in a secret. So, when it came to him showing me his love for me, it was all sexual.

Therefore, sex and anything sexual became machine-like for me. I did what I was told. I didn't know what sex was supposed to be like between two people because I had nothing to compare it to genuine love and sex. Therefore, I didn't feel that I was missing anything.

I can even say that I loved that he loved me and wanted me, and that kind of thinking had kept me stuck as his mistress. It made me feel good about myself and I loved him for it. Little did I realize that I had fallen into a trap of deception.

For the most part, Lincoln and I got along. However, it was hard to be in that "relationship." When I was at school, I was at the age when boys and girls were taking interest in each other, and I would have to make excuses why I didn't want to date anybody.

Sometimes, it was hard because I thought I loved Lincoln but still wanted to experience the dates and the socialization life of a typical teenager.

## Fined for Minor Consumption.

One night, about a month or so before school was out, I got my first minor consumption when I went out drinking with Layla and two guys, Al and Josiah. We kind of knew them but did not know their character. Layla and I were walking around town, and they stopped and asked if we wanted to go drink some beer with them, so we got in the car.

We drove around for about an hour before we found the guy they had buy them beer. Once we got some beer, we drove around drinking, stopping at a few places to see if we could drink at different people's houses but then went back to Al's house to drink since his parents weren't home.

Consequently, I came home at ten-thirty in the late evening, and I had tried to sneak in the house but my dad was waiting for me. He asked where I was, and I made up some lie. He told me to go to bed and we will talk about it in the morning.

A little while after I fell asleep, Lincoln and Chloe called. They wanted to see if I had come home because Layla still hadn't been home. I became scared because she was supposed to go home right after I went home, and she only lived a few blocks away. To make matters worse, we didn't actually know those guys.

As a result, I had to come clean about what we did that night. Lincoln and Chloe came to pick up my dad and me up to go find Layla. We went back to the house where we were drinking, and nobody was there. Then, we decided to go drive around downtown to see if we would run into them. After about an hour, we ended up spotting Layla and Al driving downtown on one of the main roads.

Lincoln went absolutely berserk. He went flying down the road alongside of them, on the wrong side of the road and cut them off the road. Then, he jumped out of the truck with a bat and pushed Al back into the seat, holding the bat against his neck, threatening him as he shouted, "If you move, it will be your worst mistake!"

Chloe and my dad got Layla out of the car, and then everybody got back into the truck. I thought we were going home, but then my dad told Lincoln to take us down to the police station so we can learn a lesson about drinking under age.

We were only two blocks away, and Lincoln lectured us the whole time. Then, while we were waiting in the hallway of the police station for an officer to come charge us, Lincoln continued to harp on us until Layla finally had enough and started to talk back to Lincoln.

Immediately, Lincoln pushed his face into hers while talking really cold and threatening her by calling her names and provoking her to do something. Layla snapped and punched him in the face. Lincoln came unglued and grabbed her around her neck squeezing with both hands to choke Layla.

We all jumped in telling Lincoln to stop. As soon as he let go, Layla became HYSTERICAL while she was crying, screaming, and punching and kicking at Lincoln.

Then the cops came out. They tried to get her to calm down, but she wouldn't. She wasn't making any sense while screaming and crying. They didn't see what had just happened, so they took it as a drunken disorderly and hauled her off to detox. Then, they wrote me out a ticket and sent us home.

The truck ride home was uncomfortably silent. My dad didn't say much when we got home either, other than he loved me and goodnight.

The next day, my dad made me get up and go to school. It was a rough day. I was grounded for a week or two at home. In addition to that, I had to go to court, pay a fine, and go to an alcohol consumption class. Layla had a fine and went to an alcohol class, too, but she didn't get punished at home, other than when Lincoln would lecture us that drinking with him was alright because we were safe. Layla and I both found him very hypocritical but wouldn't dare say that to him. So, we would appease him by agreeing just so he would drop it.

## Toxic People Have A Dominating & Jealous Nature.

Before I continue with my story, I can tell you from my personal experience that toxic people will be jealous of you and controlling, while at the same time, will try to deceive you and act like they love you. They have a victim mentality and will always make you appear to be the bad guy if you keep close relationship with them.

Therefore, if a deceiver appears to help you, his motive will be selfish to find a way to keep you to himself for his benefit and not to help you to succeed. What appears to be good is only a tool to manipulate and control you even more.

Let me explain how this continued to happen to me. After school was over for the year and I got a job working for Lincoln, I thought it was a good thing for me to get a job working with him. He worked nights at a local event center as a janitor.

Lincoln had come up with the idea of us working with him so his girls and I could make some money. First, we had to convince my dad to let this happen though. He was the one who actually talked to my dad about it. He simply told my dad that he thought it would be good for us girls to make our own money, and because of our age, it would be hard for us all to find a job.

He explained he was willing to pay us out of his check for our work. The only problem was that working at that event center required us to get up and go to work at two in the morning when the event center closed, so it would be better if I just stayed the night at their house. My dad was very unsure and didn't like that idea, but he reluctantly agreed.

After my dad agreed, I was pretty much staying the night and I did this every night of the week at Jade's and Layla's house. We drank a lot and would get little sleep, but I hung there.

Lincoln soon found out that his idea didn't go as smooth as he planned. When the first payday came around, he only got a fourth of his check. I assumed it was due to him paying out more than he expected and getting into quibbles with his daughters. For this reason, that caused him to fire them.

By him firing the girls, it ended up putting me in a really awkward position between them. I couldn't tell Lincoln I wasn't going to work with him anymore, otherwise he would freak out on me. On the other hand, Layla resented that I still had a job, making money. It started to cause friction between us.

I had to start walking this line where I tried to appease both the girls and him. The only good I had was with Jade because she was so easy going and didn't care.

The summer continued with me working nights with Lincoln, which he eventually quit paying me the amount we had initially agreed on and started paying me a lot less. However, I couldn't say anything to him about it, otherwise he would freak out on me.

On the other hand, working with Lincoln gave us much more free time together. We got along for the most part, but sometimes he would get in those weird moods where he was strictly business and would not acknowledge me on a relationship level.

I would be so confused in those periods that sometimes lasted for two to three weeks at a time. I would ask him if everything was okay and he would say, "Yeah," but his actions said differently.

Towards the end of the summer, Lincoln's brother, Jasper, showed up in the picture again. Jasper and his wife had moved back from Alabama and were living in a town close to my hometown. When he came, he usually visited on the weekends, and Lincoln, Layla, Jasper and I would go fishing and drink beer or drive around and drink beer. We played cards or darts and drank at night.

One night, a wrestling match started between everybody and continued on and off throughout the night. When everybody else went to bed, the wrestling continued between Jasper and me. At one point, Jasper pulled me down on top of him and had me straddle him and he ended up kissing me.

I was surprised and unsure of where this was going. We were both pretty drunk because we had been drinking all day.

After he kissed me, I thought I saw Jade on the stairs, watching us, but when I looked again she was gone. Then, Jasper ended up carrying me to the couch. There was an awkward fumbling between us. I sort of laid there while he stared down at me and would caress me.

I was really nervous and thinking about Lincoln. I just wasn't sure how to outright stop what was taking place. I told Jasper that I thought we shouldn't do anything. He laughed and agreed, but he continued to touch me and started to kiss on me and pulled off my pants anyway. I ended up passing out on him and am not sure of the extent of everything that was done. I was dressed when I woke up.

The next morning, I was extremely hung over, still drunk and very tired. I got up to go to work with Lincoln, and I passed back out as soon as we got into his car.

Lincoln and I were probably five miles out of town, and my dad came flying up on us. The day before that, he had told me he was coming to get me to go to church in the morning and I wasn't allowed to work that day, but I didn't think he would literally stop me from going. Finally, Lincoln pulled over on the highway, and I jumped out of his car. Without arguing, I stepped into my dad's vehicle and went back to sleep. My dad didn't bring me to church. Instead, we went home, and I went to my room and passed out again. I didn't wake up until six or seven o'clock that night.

The night before caught up to me really quick. Jade was on the stairs when Jasper had first kissed me, and she told everyone in her family about what she saw. Nobody but Lincoln said anything to me about it.

The next time we were alone, Lincoln confronted me and was

pretty nasty about it. I didn't tell him the extent of everything and just took his verbal lashings. Lincoln began calling me all sorts of names and marked his words that he would get back at me.

In the following days, Lincoln constantly flirted with his wife. He would sweet talk her, sit by her, and kiss and hug her, and would ignore me until it was just us two. Then he would talk to me again. He usually did this type of thing whenever we were in a disagreement, but this time he really laid it on heavy.

My heart literally ached. The messed up part of it was that I believed I somehow deserved what I was feeling. Because of that, I didn't say anything or respond to his verbal belittling. I just wanted things to be okay between us again. He threatened to have nothing to do with me anymore, and that scared me.

My life was completely wrapped around him and I intensely loved him. I couldn't imagine not having him. What scared me the most, was how Lincoln swore nobody else would ever love me as much as he did. Unfortunately, I believed him.

Not realizing I was in a toxic relationship being manipulated and deceived by his lies, I still was not aware that he was only using me for his selfishness. Despite the fact that he was married, he used me to make love to him and got my emotions confused and messed up.

As I have stated before, I was ignorant and did not yet label Lincoln as an abuser. I saw that continual lying was his nature while dominating and threatening me in many different ways. At that age, I didn't know that a toxic abuser will blame you for not being faithful to him and will always find ways to steal your will.

Let me go back to my story. Lincoln would never admit his wrong and his evil heart sought to manipulate, which pressured me to continually apologize to him. He controlled me in this manner and blamed me for his wrong. I never heard him apologize to me. He lived a lie with me while he pretended to love his wife when he saw her.

When Lincoln heard that Jasper had kissed me, he was mad at me for kissing Jasper, and I had apologized over and over for what happened, but he didn't let me live it down for years. We stayed together, but whenever arguments raised in our relationship, it was something that was always thrown in my face.

## For A Short Season, I Found Something I Loved Doing!

For a short season, I actually discovered some things I enjoyed in school when my eighth grade year began. That year, I did much better in school than the year before. I was in a little trouble here and there but nothing major like fighting or showing an attitude of blatant disrespect.

There were two things that I took with me from the whole eighth grade year. The first thing occurred in my English class. We were assigned a writing assignment, and I wrote a poem that my teacher thought was amazing. She sat me down and asked if she could submit it to be published in one of those books and told me that I could go somewhere with my writing.

Previously, I never knew I was good at anything until that moment, and writing has continued to be a big part of my life. It has allowed me to channel my feelings, thoughts, and creativity.

The second thing I took with me, was being part of this program in my Spanish class. Every year, the school Spanish teacher, Ms. Frieda would put on a production for the school with a famous Spanish dancer named Estrella. That year, I danced with her on stage. Besides that, I was excited to be given opportunity for a leadership role in making the program happen while preparing for this production, and I accepted that position. It felt amazing to have a purpose and watch such a beautiful thing come together. Participating in this event made me feel appreciated and gave me a purpose during that season of time.

As a result of my rewarding experience, I continued to be a part of the program and kept in contact with my Spanish teacher in the following years afterwards. I liked her beautiful spirit. She was so different in character because she actually cared for her students and wanted them to succeed in life. However, I still pursued staying in contact with Lincoln, and then things grew worse as you will read in the next chapter.

# CHAPTER 4
## Toxic Relationships Destroy Self-Esteem.

*"For rebellion is as the sin of witchcraft, and stubbornness is as iniquity and idolatry"* (I Samuel 15:23a, KJV).

Before I continue with the story about sexual abuse and the toxic relationships, I want to briefly explain what I learned much later in life, after I gave my heart to Jesus. It is not God's plan for you to lose self-esteem and feel that you are a total failure with no hope due to the terrible condemnation and manipulation from a flattering liar, a sexual abuser.

Rebellion is evil and is the nature of the devil, and God compares the work of rebellion as witchcraft and controls one's will by manipulation, condemnation, and intimidation.

Therefore, abuse of any kind defiles the will of children and adults and destroys their self-esteem with no hope or purpose in life, which makes them more rebellious. The key to freedom from a toxic relationship is to build your self-esteem through a personal encounter with Jesus Christ and letting Him be the Lord of your life.

This is why it is so important to surrender our hearts and lives to Jesus, and give him our hurts and pains. He can heal them, but we cannot.

Once you do this, He will build your self-esteem as you read the Bible, and stand on the scriptures. Then, you will no longer allow people to abuse you or control your will or life. However, I did not know the key to my freedom from abuse as yet and didn't know that abuse destroyed my self-esteem and caused me to be more rebellious to do my own thing.

Let me share something about the danger of being close to a liar. When you have a close relationship with a deceiver like Lincoln, it won't be long, and you will be following his example of lying and manipulation to get your way in other areas of your life. That's what happened to me. I would lie when I wanted to get my way, and it became worse when I dealt with others. Let me tell you this as well; it is downright frightening to see how a lie can manipulate and change the dynamics of a situation.

A lie is like wildfire and destroys whatever is in its path. In the Bible it reads, *"Likewise, the tongue is a small part of the body, but it makes great boasts. Consider what a great forest fire is set on fire by a small spark. The tongue also is a fire, a world of evil among the parts of the body. It corrupts the whole body, sets the whole course of one's life on fire, and is itself set on fire by hell"* (James 3:5-6, NIV).

### Lies Spread Like Wild Fire.

Let me continue with my story. At one point during my eighth grade year, my dad became fed up with my actions of always wanting to go to Jade's and Layla's home, and then coming home late, which was past my curfew.

However, I felt that being late was not my fault, and deep-down, I blamed Lincoln because he always messed around before he dropped me off at my home. It bugged me that he didn't care if I was disciplined for being late.

Because of being late, my dad started to put his foot down. He said that I couldn't go over to Jade's and Layla's home as much, and then he tried to stop me entirely. I freaked out when he tried stopping me entirely, and I was mad at him. To rebel against his decisions, I lied and told Lincoln and Chloe that my dad hit me. I wasn't sure what would happen when I lied, but I regretted it moments after I told it.

As a result of my lie, Lincoln and Chloe contacted social services. Chloe was concerned, but Lincoln wanted me to get emancipated so I could permanently live with them. I wasn't sure what I started. I didn't know how to turn back my steps and tell the truth. Speaking the truth was actually more complicated than just me lying about it because it was about what I was protecting.

Afterwards, Lincoln contacted my mom who lived in a town an hour north and told her about what was happening. Also, he told her to come and get me. My mom contacted her attorney, and at that point, my dad was already contacted by social services. I couldn't imagine how my dad was feeling.

When my dad came home from work that night, it was really awkward. My dad didn't ask me why I lied, and he didn't even yell at me. He asked me if I wanted to stay with my mom, and I told him, "Yes!" It wasn't what I really wanted, but I couldn't stand the feeling of being so ashamed and having to be by him after what I had done. The next day, my mom came to get me and brought me back to her house.

At first, living with her wasn't so bad because Lincoln, Jade, and Layla came frequently to see me. Jade and Layla actually stayed quite a few nights with me, but they were sent home once I started acting up when not listening to my mom. They came back the next day though, and Lincoln and Jasper drank some beers and visited with my mom to get her back in good graces.

When Lincoln left to pick up Chloe from work and Jasper had to head home, my mom went with them because they were going to bar hop on the way back. Without my mom knowing, Lincoln ended up leaving us girls some beer, so we sat drinking and watching movies at mom's house.

After about a week or more of living at my mom's house, my dad called and told me he was coming to get me. My mom was furious, but I was sort of relieved because I was feeling awfully depressed with what I had done. I wasn't wanting to start a new life or a new school.

When I went home, we had a counselor come see us once a week to do in-home family counseling. It went well. Again, Lincoln told me what to say and how to "play the game" to appease them to get them to stop coming around.

At that time, my dad was stricter on me. There were no more sleepovers during the week and only one on the weekend. I was reluctant but accepted it because I didn't have a choice.

## Life Gets Worse
## With Toxic Relationships.

During the fall season, it was the first time I heard people having suspicions of Lincoln and me. My brother, Asher, had married, and after the church ceremony, the reception was held at a local bar. The reception was going really great. Everyone was dancing and conversing. Lincoln was buying *Windsor Cokes* for me and Layla, and we would drink on the down low.

Towards the end of the night when everything was dwindling, talk begin to spread about Lincoln and me. While in the bathroom, one of our really good family friends told me and Layla that my brothers, Everett and Asher, thought something weird was going on between Lincoln and me. That stunned me and fear hit me. Then, because I was drinking, I blew it way out of proportion, became hysterical and confronted them.

My brothers said, "Yeah we said it," but I could tell they weren't wanting to talk about it right then. I had still demanded to know why they would say that, and to appease my hysterics they both said they thought it was weird that I was always with him.

Immediately, I denied anything happening. I had no clue what Lincoln was doing while I was talking to them. Then we left after the situation was defused.

Afterwards, Lincoln threw an after-party, wedding party, at his house. A few people showed up and drank some more. Nothing more was said that night about Lincoln and me. It wasn't brought up in the days that followed either, so I figured I would let it go. There was no sense in poking a sleeping bear.

Occasionally, both of my older brothers hung out with Lincoln. They both were within ten years younger than Lincoln. Many times they hung out to go fishing together and also would drink with Lincoln. They knew that Lincoln would give me and his girls alcohol. They didn't say much about it, after Lincoln explained to them he would rather us drink at home with him than going out and getting into trouble.

When the ninth grade started, Jade, Layla, and I decided to go to a different school in a nearby town. We wanted a fresh start together. I liked the new school. The school was even smaller than our old school. The whole ninth grade was in one class, and everybody pretty much got along.

In the mornings, we usually rode the bus and Lincoln would usually pick us up in the evenings. We thought it was awesome because he would usually have cigarettes and beer waiting for us to enjoy on the drive home. I would have to be home by supper, so I couldn't drink that much. However, if I had my chores done, my dad would let me go back to hang out with Jade and Layla until curfew, and then I would drink some more.

Not long into the new school year, a friend of ours was shot in a hunting accident. He was from a few years back at our old school. Even though none of us hadn't talked to him in a couple years, it was still rattling. He was such a nice guy; it seemed so surreal.

Chloe, Jade, Layla and I went to the funeral. After the funeral, our new friend from school, Hazel, and Layla, and I went with Lincoln, Jasper, and my brother, Asher, driving around drinking beer on the back gravel roads. When we started seeing a bunch of deer, we went back to town and got more beer and Lincoln and Jasper got their guns.

Before we left again, there was a big scene between Lincoln and Chloe because Lincoln had his shotgun, and Chloe was trying to take it away. She was also yelling at us girls to get out of the truck. She didn't want us going because we were just at a funeral for a kid who was accidentally shot, but Lincoln told us to stay in the truck. They exchanged some words. In not so nice words, Lincoln yelled at Chloe to get in the house. Afterwards, Lincoln got into the vehicle and we all left.

The night was very intense. We drove around drinking and shooting at different things. Jasper was driving and would try to chase down deer with his blazer. We were hopping ditches at dangerous speeds that threw us all over the blazer and speeding through fields. There were times when I was actually scared because they did not have safety in mind.

Later that night, Lincoln started to get frisky with me and was very reckless. He was putting his hand up my shirt and kissing on me, while Layla, Hazel, Lincoln and I all sat in the backseat. Then Layla saw him put his hand up my shirt. I tried to block it and let Lincoln know to chill out, but he blew it off and would continue to grab on me throughout the night.

Layla quit talking to me the rest of the night. When we got home, she ran upstairs to her room with Hazel and told her and Jade the things she saw. Jade came to talk to me about it and I denied it. I felt so bad for lying to her, too. I went downstairs and told Lincoln how angry Layla was, and he told me not to worry about it. I walked back upstairs and passed out.

Sometime during the night, I woke up with Layla standing over me with a pair of scissors. I was completely freaked out. She said nothing, threw the scissors at me and ran back upstairs. Needless to say, I did not sleep well the rest of the night. I was really unsure of what her intentions were with those scissors.

The next day, I rose up early and told Jade and Lincoln what had happened, and I still had the scissors. They both were surprised but Lincoln laughed it off, pretty much telling me to let it go because we all knew how Layla could get.

I went home and wanted to stay away for a while, but that was impossible because Layla, Jade, and I had school together. We were transported together, and Lincoln and Jade had wanted me to come around. It was uncomfortable though.

Layla was only mad at me and not Lincoln, so I felt like I was an elephant in the room because they all conversed and went on with things as usual. Whenever I was included in the conversation, there was this cold shoulder coming from Layla, which everybody saw but said nothing.

Shortly after that, Layla came back around and talked to me again after Lincoln had talked to her, but things weren't the same. She watched Lincoln and I like a hawk. Whenever we all would be drinking, she would be very passively aggressive, mostly towards me but just in general, too. It was just something I had to ignore.

Then one night, not too long after we all went driving around, Lincoln, Jasper, Asher, Layla, Hazel and I were all drinking at the house. Soon, Asher invited our Dad to come over, so Layla, Hazel, and I would have to go upstairs to have a beer or a cigarette, which wasn't that big of deal.

Everything was going fine until Lincoln and Jasper started teaming up to pick on Asher. At first they were joking, but then Lincoln and Jasper got mean about it. The situation escalated to the point of them almost fighting and it probably would have if my Dad wasn't there to just have Asher leave.

After that night, Asher didn't really ever talk to Lincoln and Jasper again. Lincoln and Jasper would sit and bad talk him when they got super drunk to the point that it was annoying. I would try to defend Asher sometimes, but then they turned on me. For this reason, I just had to ignore it to keep the negativity to a minimum.

At that time, I did not understand the difference between toxic and healthy relationships. Living with toxic people would always lead me into further darkness and devastation. You will find it will always lead into shame and one trauma after another and make you feel helpless and hopeless. However, my eyes were still spiritually blind in this matter of understanding.

## Toxic Relationships
## Make You Feel Cold & Dirty!

Jackson, Jade, and Layla's brother, and I had been really good friends for a while at this point, but he had started asking me to go out with him. He had always liked me but hadn't pursued me until then. He wrote me beautiful love letters pouring out his heart. They were so enduring but left me feeling horrible because I knew nothing could happen between us. Even if I were to leave Lincoln, he would not allow us to be together.

I told Lincoln about the letters when Jackson first started writing them, and he didn't really say too much. After I received a few, Lincoln wanted to see them. So one day, I gave them to him when we were out working at a lake.

Lincoln sat and read them while we were waiting for some brush to burn off, but when he was done, he burned them too. I was so mad, but I couldn't say anything without Lincoln getting mad at me. I just didn't ever give him the letters that Jackson continued to write. Face-to-face, Jackson even started telling me how much he loved me, and it would kill me to reject him.

Furthermore, I loved Lincoln, but I always questioned his love towards me because he went in phases at times and would ignore me. The only time he wanted anything thing to do with me during these periods, was when he wanted me sexually. Even then he wouldn't say much and kept it straight to the point, which was something sexual. Sometimes, I would silently cry during our encounters because I didn't feel loved. The contact felt so cold and dirty.

Afterwards, Lincoln would drop me off at home with little words, and I would go to my room and hope that tomorrow would be better.

The mental bewilderment was the difference he could make when he came around. On one hand, I believed in Lincoln's sick way he loved me, even if it was only at times. He would vow he would do anything for me by saying he would "treat me like a queen." When we would have supper, he would make me a plate and bring it to me. Also, he would buy me cigarettes and beer, and he would hug on me, kiss me, rub on me, and profess how much I meant to him. He would make me a priority.

In another way, Lincoln would map out my steps and tell me what to do with my life. He seduced me in such a way that made it sound "happily ever after." His seduction would have me floating on clouds, and I was gullible to believe in everything he was selling. I would get this hopeful feeling that he wouldn't ever ignore me again.

Then again, he never kept his flattering promises. He kept me confused and deceived as I believed his lies, and the "pretend love" he had for me when he was just cold, which occurred in cycles. It was not real, but I played his game with him for many seasons.

However, it was my dream and desire to have a relationship with a man who loved me and proved it. With Jackson, I knew he loved me by the way he looked at me, talked to me, treated me, and he went out of his way for me. We would sit and talk to each other for hours. He would try to teach me to play a guitar, and we would play games, cards, darts, and hackie-sack or go on walks. Our friendship was real.

As a result, I ended up messing around with Jackson without going too far one night. I knew I was crossing a line that Lincoln would eventually find out about, but it was one of those "in the moment" type of things.

Because of that, I had to end it as soon as Jackson told Lincoln, because, of course, Lincoln flipped out, but I didn't really care this time. I knew I had it coming. It crushed Jackson but he accepted it. I just told him I wasn't interested in a relationship at this point. Our friendship hadn't changed at all. We continued to hang out like we always did.

Eventually, he moved on and started dating a really good girl. I was genuinely happy for him.

After that, going to our new school didn't last long. Jade ended up getting into a conflict with some girls who were once our friends. For some reason, they didn't like Jade being with her new boyfriend, so they started some drama. You know high school!

Anyway, I thought we were going to fight with one of the girls' older sisters, so I brought my pepper spray to school just in case. I had it for a while and I wanted to see if it worked. That was when I sprayed it in an empty locker. It affected the kids in school. The whole top floor of the school was coughing. I guess it worked, but someone told on me and I was kicked out of school for two weeks.

When I went back to school, a fight started out between Jade and one of the girls, so we ended up leaving the new school. So much for the fresh start.

## Fined for Minor Alcohol Consumption.

Afterwards, we started going to a private school in my hometown. I loved this school. We only went from eight to ten o'clock every morning. We worked at our own pace in a class size of six to eight of us. The teachers were really nice and seemed to really want us to succeed.

When we weren't at school, most of the time Layla, Lincoln, Jackson and I would be drinking. We would drive around and drink, go shoot guns somewhere and drink. In the winter, we would ice fish and drink, and we would sit in the garage and play darts and drink. We were always drinking with whatever we were doing.

I knew I was becoming an alcoholic and it scared me. I wasn't sure how to get a handle on it, but I thought that one day I would eventually be able to face the issue and overcome it. Not too often I would wake shaking and have to drink a beer to just stop.

Many times, we were drinking by eleven o clock in the morning. I would have to go easy on my drinking until after I would go home and have supper with my family. Then, if I got to go back out again, which I usually did, I would get more to drink. Lincoln always called it playing the game, which meant doing what I need to do to keep the attention off me and appease whoever I needed to please them. I did do pretty well at it, but eventually I got caught.

One night, I went home drunk and fell against the wall. Asher and his wife were there. My dad straight out asked me if I had been drinking. I replied, "No!" Then, he took me to the hallway and shined a light in my eyes. Because my pupils didn't dilate, he said he was calling the cops.

At the time, we had dial up internet and Asher was sitting on the computer, so my dad went out to his truck to grab his cell phone. As he was coming back in and through the garage, I ran out the front door. It was dark, and I ran behind the house cutting through back yards of our neighbors. I could hear my dad yelling my name, madder than all get out.

I was maybe two houses over and hit a clothes line that literally clothes-lined me. My feet flew up over my head, and I landed on my back; it knocked the wind out of me. I couldn't lay there too long because I could still hear my dad yelling. Then, I got up and started running again until I ran my forehead into a pine tree branch and I fell again.

Eventually, I made it back to Lincoln's home, but a cop was waiting down the street. My dad told them where I was headed, so they cuffed me and brought me home. They said they were only going to ticket me for underage consumption and told me to go in and get some sleep.

The next morning, I woke up with the inside of my cheek split from clothes lining myself, a lump on my forehead from running into the tree branch, and a hangover. My dad grounded me, needless to say.

## More About the Jealous Nature of Lincoln.

Jade and Layla ended up going through a phase where they didn't want anything to do with me. Their attitude made it very awkward for me because Lincoln still wanted me to come over, but the girls didn't want me around.

Layla and I still hadn't fully recovered a good friendship after that one night she saw her dad's hand up my shirt. She started hacking my email back when Hotmail was very easy to get into someone else's account, and she would change my password. After she had locked me out of my email, at three different times, I finally changed hers and she flipped a switch over it.

We started arguing about it, until Lincoln punched a hole in the wall telling us to shut up. I got up to leave and Jackson gave me a ride home.

Jade stopped talking to me after that night, and I am not really sure why she stopped. I stayed home for a good week or two and only talked to Jackson, and occasionally, I talked to Lincoln. The solitude was actually kind of nice because I didn't feel the demands I usually felt in living up to the expectations of Lincoln.

Also, I experienced some anxiety though. Every once in a while, I couldn't breathe and had no clue what was happening to me. I realized how much my life was wrapped around Lincoln, and without him I have nothing left. The realization shook me.

I had let go of every friend I had before, even friendships I had since being a toddler. I also didn't have much of a relationship with any of my family anymore, and I had no life and no pastime activities. To top it off, I had also developed a drinking problem, and I had no way to drink at home.

All I had was my two school hours in the morning. Jackson would bring me to school, and after school I did my homework. Then, I would bring all my work home and do homework for hours to keep my mind occupied.

I spent my sixteenth birthday alone, besides a few hours with Jackson. He came over and brought me a gift, which was a black hills gold ring and forty bucks. Then, we went out driving the country roads for a while. It was such a pretty fall day. I didn't want to go home, but he had to go to work, so I went home and spent the evening with my family.

Then, I went deer hunting with my dad. It was nice to bond like that. I hadn't realized how far we had drifted apart until we started spending quality time together again. My dad is one of those guys that is so unconditionally supportive of his kids. He would always tell us kids, "I don't always love what you do, but I will always love you." It was a confession that made us feel grateful and ashamed at the same time. Besides that, he believed in tough love, and though some trials were hard to go through, I knew he parented out of love and did the best he could.

Jade started talking to me about two weeks later. She needed help finding a place in town, and she and Lincoln came to get me so I could show them. I guess Lincoln had talked to her to get her to forgive what upset her. Then, Jade had come around, and we started hanging out again.

Not long after that, Jackson loaned me the money to go to school to become a certified nursing assistant. I also ended up graduating high school at sixteen. When I was grounded or had to stay at home, I would work on my school work and was able to work ahead that way.

Once I graduated, I ended up working a couple nursing jobs, but my drinking got in the way of both. As summer came around, I started working with Lincoln again.

Actually, Lincoln, Jackson, Layla, Jade and I all started working together remodeling an old school house a lady bought. The job was fun and flexible, and we were paid good and got to drink.

We actually landed this job from Lincoln's friend who he knew from his hometown and moved around the area. His name was Cyrus. He was in his late twenties. He was tall with blonde hair and blue eyes.

Shortly after we began this project, I started catching Cyrus looking at me playfully. While he was working inside and I was outside doing landscaping, I would look up as he would be in the window watching me and smile when I caught him.

When we were taking breaks or working on smaller projects, he would continue to look at me. After work, we would all go hang out and drink, and I would still catch him staring at me.

Then one day I had to go home because we had family visiting and I left Lincoln walking. When I made it down the block and around the corner, Cyrus came pulling up and offered me a ride. I got in and there was silence for a minute.

With curiosity, I asked him why he keeps looking at me the way he did. His answer was, "I like you!" The conversation progressed, and we agreed to a plan to meet that night. I took down his number. He was another *Smoosher*!

That night, I told my dad I was going to babysit. To make it look legit, I had him drive me to the apartment complexes to drop me off there. Then after he drove off, I walked the rest of the way to where I was supposed to meet Cyrus. We ended up meeting like this quite regularly for the next couple weeks. We would either go back to his house or drive around to drink and fool around before he would bring me back home.

One night, Cyrus asked me if I would pack up and leave to move away with him. The idea sounded scary but also intriguing to start a whole new life somewhere. I thought about it. As much as I wasn't caring too much for Lincoln at the moment because he was going through one of his phases, it scared me to be without him. Therefore, I didn't really give Cyrus an answer.

The next time I decided to see Cyrus, I snuck out of our house and my dad went upstairs for something and noticed I wasn't home. He called Jade's and Layla's house to see if I was there, and when I wasn't, he called the cops.

My dad, Lincoln, Jackson, and the cops were all looking for me. That night, Cyrus and I happened to be out driving around drinking, and he dropped me off about three in the morning. It wasn't until the next morning when I found out that everyone was looking for me.

I first became awake when my dad was asking me where I went last night and I made up a story. Then he left me alone and I went back to sleep.

On the second time, I woke up to Lincoln. My dad had already gone to work. Lincoln had helped himself into the house, which wasn't unusual for him to do, and he woke me up and demanded to know where I was and I lied to him, also. Lincoln said it was kind of ironic that Cyrus wasn't home either and put this theory together about Cyrus and me. I still denied being with Cyrus. I guess Lincoln had already talked to Cyrus who said he had gone back to their hometown for the night.

Lincoln didn't believe me and hounded me for a while after that, but I didn't ever tell him anything different. I also saw a new side to him, too. I think he realized I was not that little girl anymore that was just going to follow him around waiting for the slightest bit of attention.

After that, he treated me differently. He started to treat me more like a girlfriend and inquire more how I felt or wanted to do. He included me and wanted me by his side. We tried starting a new chapter. He started taking just me out to do things like go fishing or driving around, and things were really good for a while.

I ended up getting my driver's license, and I helped Ms. Frieda with another Spanish program. We had a lot of fun getting that production together, and it happened to be my little sister's year for the Spanish program, so I got to bond with her, too. Before that, I didn't really have anything to do with her.

### The Danger I Suffered For Not Obeying My Parents.

Throughout my childhood and teen years, I went through much adversity, troubles, and suffering due to lying to my parents and not obeying them. There is a reason why God gives children the instruction to obey their parents and not rebel against them.

In the Bible, we read an excellent scripture that says, *"My Son, keep your father's command and do not forsake your mother's teaching"* (Proverbs 6:20, NIV). If I would have obeyed my dad's instruction and tell him the truth and listened to my mom, I could have been protected from a tremendous amount of unnecessary abuse and hardship as a child and teenager.

Let me clarify some things and give you a better view of my

parents and the dynamics concerning me and them. A common question I have heard people asking me when telling people my story is, "Where were your parents?" My parents were there, but they were fooled.

Lincoln coached me on what to say concerning many instances. When I would drink before going home, I had to wash up or shower, brush my teeth, and change my clothes to mask the alcohol. Also, Lincoln usually pulled the alcohol an hour before I had to be home. When my family started suspecting something weird going on, my dad straight out asked me if there was something going on between Lincoln and me, and I denied everything.

As stated previously, before I graduated school, my dad limited my time over at Layla's and Jade's home. My dad put a lot of faith of me, and I sadly lied and took advantage of it for a long time. I went to school two hours a day and had all day to do whatever behind his back. After that, I got my nursing assistant license and took a night shift briefly, so that gave me plenty of leeway to lie about going to work, especially when I no longer had the job.

However, I regret not listening to my father and not following him in his teachings. Following Lincoln's way had lead me straight to hell on earth.

My parents were good parents that took time to instill good morals even though I did not really have a relationship with my mother ever since I sabotaged her custody battle. She still tried as well.

On the other hand, Lincoln was a master manipulator and nobody knew what Lincoln was up too, even his own wife, when it was happening right under her nose. Lincoln dominated my morals and freewill by playing on my naive nature. His actions caused great damage and it was really hard to not blame myself because I was lying right along with him.

I couldn't forgive myself until much later after I got free from Lincoln. It wasn't until I got married and had my own children and realized that complete agape love, which parents have for their children. Due to being able to witness the innocents of children growing up, I was able to forgive myself, and I realize that I was manipulated and brainwashed into believing false love.

In conclusion of this section, I do not blame my parents for not protecting me. Their trust was taken advantage of, just as much as mine was by Lincoln.

However, I do think this situation can be used as a wise lesson to put into perceptive that children and adolescents growing into their teenage years don't have the wisdom or knowledgeable insight to see the full scope of circumstances that adults see. So, unfortunately it doesn't take much to manipulate them.

As parents, we need to raise our children to be firm in Christ, knowing all the rights and wrongs and not leave openings for other deceivers to give the devil a foothold to steal, kill, and destroy. Trusting adults can be manipulated by other deceiving adults every day. Therefore, think of how easily it can happen to children. For this reason, having open and honest communication is vital. Children are only as safe as we keep them.

To conclude this chapter, I want to say that a deer doesn't lose its spots overnight. In other words, if you have been a victim of abuse, an abuser just doesn't change overnight, and you will be continually controlled like a puppet. Only having the courage to leave will free you. You will read more about this in the next chapters.

# Chapter 5
## Strongholds Are Hard To Cut.

*"But a man who commits adultery has no sense; whoever does so destroys himself. Blows and disgrace are his lot, and his shame will never be wiped away"* (Proverbs 6:32-33, NIV).

In this chapter, I will discuss the struggle I suffered to cut ties of being involved in a toxic relationship with Lincoln. I was in a battle for my life, and still I was ignorant that he was being used by the devil to control my decisions and steal, kill, and destroy my hope to succeed in life.

A controlling deceiver is like a python snake. He will first act like he is attracted to you, but he will eventually constrict you and squeeze the life out of you until you feel helpless and forced to let him destroy your will in life.

Deceivers only keep their own interest in mind and don't ever consider the other persons. Healthy relationships are a bond between two people that keep each other's interest in minds and doing what is right and just for the whole family.

Another thing abusers will do, is get you in a position to control and restrict you from having a healthy relationship with others.

The Bible warns us that an adulterer is destroying his own soul and will have a wound and dishonor, and his reproach and shame will not be wiped away but will torment him. Eventually, this sin will take him to hell if he won't repent and won't get his heart and life right with God.

In the Bible, Jesus said that the devil is your enemy to steal and destroy your life. *"The thief comes only in order to steal and kill and destroy. I came that they may have and enjoy life, and have it in abundance [to the full, till it overflows]"* (John 10:10, AMP). In that scripture, Jesus said that He will not lie, manipulate, or deceive you, but He came to give you abundant life to enjoy His joy and peace and all His wonderful benefits on earth and eternally in Heaven.

I did not know that God had a great plan and purpose for my life and getting sexually involved with Lincoln was not God's plan. Because I was in spiritual blindness, I fell into a trap.

Eventually, I wanted to get out of it, and I tried various ways to leave Lincoln. If you are stuck with a sexual abuser, or any other type of abuser, I want you to know that Jesus has a great plan for your life. Jesus loves you and has plans for you to succeed in life and live in abundant joy, peace, and victory in all areas of your life.

Therefore, you don't have to suffer anymore guilt, shame, lies, and torment from a sexual abuser. You don't have to keep going down the road to destruction like I did when I was ignorant and unlearned in this area. Being forced into a sexual encounter and close relationship with an abuser who manipulates your emotions and will, is not the nature of God, but it is the plan of the devil to destroy your life.

It is not God's plan for you to continually suffer with the weight of guilt and shame, which leads to torment, thinking you are the blame for sexual abuse and feeling you are stuck and can't get out. This creates more confusion and will make you feel obligated to fix his toxic nature and problems with no concern for yourself.

God's plan is to be free from abuse and live in the peace of God that comes when you follow God's Word. How awesome it is that Jesus will take our yoke, which consists of problems, pains, faults, and whatever, and give us His yoke that is light and easy, and is forever and eternal, good and humble! The Bible says it this way, *"Come to me, all you who are weary and burdened, and I will give you rest. Take my yoke upon you and learn from me, for I am gentle and humble in heart, and you will find rest for your souls. For my yoke is easy and my burden is light"* (Matthew 11:28-30, NIV).

We are beyond blessed! All He wants from us is to live out His instructions of being kind, humble, selfless, loving, and forgiving.

Another way to look at it is this. Jesus took our place. He died on the cross and rose from the dead so we don't have to suffer from our misfortunes, mistakes, and faults throughout life and be condemned to hell. Therefore, if we continue to live in suffering, then that means Jesus died for nothing!

Moving on, because I was in a spiritual blindness, I was not aware that the devil's tools and weapons would lead me into more confusion and destruction in my life. Eventually, it led me to alcohol and drug abuse, which led to even more destruction.

To cut ties with an abuser, you can only be successful when you can fully see your abuser as a disturbed human being who only thinks of his own interests and uses you to satisfy himself.

I tried to cut ties with Lincoln, but I didn't ever find freedom from the abuse until years later when I was introduced to God.

So, in the meantime, I kept falling deeper in the muck and mire of unhealthy relationships. Your freedom begins when you give your heart to Jesus, confess your sin of being hooked to an abuser, read the Bible, and make a step to change in the right direction.

## The Struggle of Cutting Ties With A Sexually Toxic Relationship.

When we are closely bonded to an abuser in a sexual relationship and keep going back, it's because of the lack of self-esteem and self-worth. If we become so beaten down and tired emotionally, it's hard to believe we are worth more than the situation we continue to live in. It makes it easy to find ourselves in a big struggle of confusion and hopelessness.

Not only does it drain you emotionally, abuse makes you mentally and physically worn out and drains the life out of you. To escape my problems, I drank heavily.

Many feel alone, lost, and without love and hope when they try to leave the abuser. As in my case, he will try all kinds of manipulative

## Chapter 5. Strongholds Are Hard To Cut.

tactics to control your mind and will and make you feel guilty and also obligated to be with him. This is what happened in my life when I tried to leave Lincoln at seventeen.

I will share the following details of my story to help other people in similar situations to avoid this continual devastating trauma that really wastes precious years of a person's life.

Things appeared to get better when I had my first real job working in healthcare. I learned to really like and appreciate that job. I actually liked the people and the clients I worked with. I worked part-time but usually got full-time hours by picking up other shifts.

Everything was going really well until I started working with a guy named Quinton. He was different from the other guys I had known. He actually had goals and hobbies that didn't involve continual partying.

One morning, we began talking on the subject of drinking, and I told him I could probably out drink him. He didn't think there was any way possible and his logic was his size. He was really tall and three-hundred pounds of muscle, and I was five feet and five inches tall, weighing one-hundred and twenty pounds.

Well, we shook hands and agreed the loser had to buy the other a case of beer. It was about a week later when my brother, Sawyer, was going into the national guards for training. Therefore, Pippa and I were going to go party with him before he left. I had to tell Lincoln it was a family function to avoid an argument of me wanting to party with Sawyer.

Then I was talking to Quinton and told him he should come up, and we will compete to see who could out drink the other. The night turned out to be super fun. I enjoyed drinking with them and was happy I was away from Lincoln. I didn't have him policing everything I did or said.

Pippa got drunk for her first time and ended up puking. Halfway through the night, Quinton slipped and fell down the stairs and passed out shortly after the fall. I continued to stay up drinking for a while after that, until I passed out on the floor.

The next morning, Quinton woke me to tell me he was leaving, and all I said was, "I won," and went back to sleep. I had to work later that afternoon and it was rough. I didn't usually stay up drinking until four or five in the morning, and I had to get Lincoln's car back.

I went to work, and when I got off, Quinton called me and said he was going back to drink with my brother, Sawyer, and wanted me to go with them. I told Lincoln that my dad wanted me to come home that night, but he didn't seem to mind so much because his friend was watching his nephews at Lincoln's place.

I went home and Quinton and his friend picked me up, not that long after I got home. We headed to my brothers' place again. We drank for a while. Then, Quinton wanted to go drive around.

Therefore, his friend drove us to Quinton's house where we traded out vehicles. Afterwards, we drove around the backroads drinking and talking. He told me all about his marriage and kids, but then he told me the marriage wasn't going so well. After sharing that, he asked me out and I accepted.

I was looking forward to the change. I wanted to have a relationship where I could be completely open with somebody. I just had to figure out how I could leave Lincoln. It wasn't easy. I was mostly scared of how Lincoln was going to react. In the meantime, I just had to give Quinton excuses explaining why I couldn't spend time with him when he wanted to take me out.

Then one night, Quinton and I had plans to go out and drink. I told Lincoln that I was working overnight at the group homes, and Jackson brought me a change of clothes and a toothbrush.

Then I told my brother, Everett, and also Quinton, that my car wouldn't start. I proceeded to tell them to just come pick me up. I was trying to avoid Lincoln. So, if he would drive by to check up on me like he often did, he would think I was still there.

## Chapter 5. Strongholds Are Hard To Cut.

We ended up drinking at my dad's place. My dad finally allowed me to have a few beers when Sawyer went off to National Guards. I think it was because I was with Quinton who was older and responsible and he thought I was making better decisions.

After a few hours, Quinton and I went back to his house to crash. I had him set his alarm for eight-thirty in the morning so I could be back to my car by nine o'clock to make it look like I had gotten off work at the time I should have.

However, that is not what happened. When morning came around, we didn't wake up until ten-thirty to eleven o'clock in the morning. I was feeling rough, and I was hoping I could get to my car to Lincoln's home without much attention drawn and questions asked about where I was.

My hope was quickly diminished and replaced with trouble as soon as I walked into Lincoln's house. I was bombarded with questions and mean mugs about where I had been and what I had been doing. I lied and said I was with my friend Samantha who lived a block down from my dad's house and lied about working so I could go drink with her.

Then Lincoln said, "Oh, yeah! What about Quinton?" Inside I felt my whole body stiffen, but I said, "What are talking about?"

Furthermore, Lincoln went on to elaborate that when I didn't come home by nine-thirty, they were worried and Jackson went to my work to see what I was doing. He was told I didn't work that night, and they began questioning why I left my car and my purse was in it.

So, they started going around everywhere they knew to find me. They stopped by Samantha's place and was told that she was in school. Afterwards, they drove to the college and left a note on her car to call them.

Then, Lincoln said they went down to my dad's work and asked him if they had seen me, and my dad said really smug-like, "Oh, Amy? She's with Quinton!"

I assumed that Lincoln went home and found out where Quinton lived and was over at his house knocking on the door while we were upstairs sleeping and was peeking into the garage and house because he had seen a corvette in the garage.

He thought that Quinton was into drugs and whatever else to afford a corvette, so I used his assumption to my advantage. I said that Everett and Quinton were friends and he had stopped by my dad's house while Samantha and I stopped in and we all left at the same time, and he must have thought I was with him. He bought the story somewhat, but I could tell he didn't fully trust me.

Then Chloe, Lincoln's wife, needed to go to class an hour away, and Lincoln asked if I was riding with him while he drove her up there. I didn't want to, but I didn't think I should say no, especially when I don't hardly ever stay back unless I was working. Jade was going also, so that was my only comfort of not hearing him bash me the whole time Chloe was in class.

The whole way there, Lincoln was slamming beers and playing the new *Korn* song over and over. There was a line in there about betrayal that he was very vocal about. Meanwhile, he would talk very sweet to Chloe. Every once in a while, I could feel him glaring at me through the rearview mirror. That was the longest trip ever. He didn't say one word to me. I could tell he just had me along as part of his control. I plotted my way out the whole trip.

After we came back to town, I told Lincoln that I needed to go to the bank. He seemed worried I was leaving and followed me outside. Then, Lincoln made sure I was coming back and I could see his thoughts going.

I got into my car, drove away, and skipped going to the bank, for I already had cash on me. That was just a lie to buy a couple minutes to get away from Lincoln.

I went straight to my dad's work and said, "Dad, I don't want you to ask me any questions. Just please do what I ask without hesitation. When I leave, wait five minutes and call the cops, and tell them you

## Chapter 5. Strongholds Are Hard To Cut.

want your underage daughter to come home, and send them over to Jade and Layla's house to escort me home. Make sure you tell them to have me pack up all my belongings before I go, too." He said he would, so I left and went back to see Lincoln.

When I arrived back to Lincoln's house, I had just sat down on the front step outside and lit my cigarette, and I saw the cops come around the corner. Lincoln was sitting outside with me and was trying to make small talk. When he saw them, I could see panic across his face while wondering what was happening.

As they approached us, they said exactly what I had asked my dad to tell them. Lincoln was in complete disbelief. I could see that he was beside himself not knowing what to do. I went in and packed up my things and put the bags into my car. When I was done, I told the cops I was just going to say goodbye and then I would leave. So, they left.

I went inside to say goodbye, but while I was in there, my brother Everett, called and asked, "Amy, are you coming home?" Quickly I replied, "Yeah!" Then Lincoln grabbed the phone from me and was trying to tell Everett what my dad was doing, but he was quickly shut down. Everett asked Lincoln what he was doing, and then proceeded to tell Lincoln to let me come home. In more or less words, Everett said I belonged to his family and not Lincoln's family.

After that, Lincoln lost it. He screamed into the phone, "That's my baby girl. I raised her! She belongs to me!"

Then Everett laughed at him. The voice of Lincoln went cold and threatened him saying, "Watch your back, Everett. When you least expect it, you will be walking outside at night and I will pick you off from over a hundred yards away. You won't even see it coming."

Meanwhile, Everett didn't take it seriously, but I did. I knew Lincoln could be ruthless. I started to wonder where this was going to lead, but I just had to get out of there. Quickly, I grabbed my phone and left.

When I was home, I felt somewhat relieved. I was looking forward to my new start and seeing what would become of Quinton and me. I really liked him. He was so easy going and got along well with all my family. I couldn't help but think this is what I have always wanted to have someone and a relationship. I didn't have to hide and we can be around my family.

It didn't take long to realize I still had to hide Quinton. I told him to not say anything because the daughter of Lincoln, Layla, worked at one of the houses, and I didn't want her going back and telling Lincoln.

This led to him being puzzled, and he asked why I was worried if Lincoln found out. I said it was because I was only seventeen, and I didn't want our relationship to start trouble. Actually, I was very scared of Lincoln and what he would do if he found out the reason I left and was seeing someone else.

At first, I had a very limited communication with Lincoln when he would try to contact me. He started to carry a cell phone, which he never used one before and would call and text me all the time. I tried to get him to back off by responding with a brief text message stating that dad was monitoring my calls and texts.

However, his text messages did get to me. They made me feel like a really awful person, as though I was the blame for his depression and discouragement. I heard the hurt in the voice of Lincoln. He was upset that I was not there with him.

Sometimes when I went to work, I would swing by and have a cigarette with him. In just the few days I was gone, he looked horrible as though he hadn't been sleeping and just drinking. The color of his skin was greyish and he hadn't showered in a while. I was concerned.

One evening, Quinton and I were hanging out with my dad in the living room. It was a pretty slow evening with not a lot happening. We visited and watched some television.

Then we went out to the garage where Everett was hanging out partying. We sat there drinking a few beers, listening to music, and watching Everett hang up things on the garage walls.

## Chapter 5. Strongholds Are Hard To Cut.

The next morning when I stopped to see Lincoln, he started telling me things that happened the previous night at my dad's house, and I was so taken back by it. Then, when he pretty much recited how the whole night went, I was shocked.

Furthermore, he continued to say that he was at the house watching through the windows and saw me laughing and having a good time. He said he stood two feet away from Everett and felt like pulling the trigger.

Lincoln proceeded to tell me that Layla and his brother, Jasper, were with him, and he borrowed Jasper's pistol to hold onto it for a while. A sense of doom hit me. I had to quickly come up with a reason to explain why I hung out with everyone and why I was not upstairs as I had previously told Lincoln, which was where I usually hung out.

Immediately, I told him that all I did was work and sat upstairs and watched movies, but I occasionally went down to spend time with the family, and if I didn't, I would go stir crazy. He wasn't persuaded by what I said, and he had an adverse attitude about it.

Not knowing what would happen, I started shaking inside with fear and I hurried back home in panic. I let my family know what Lincoln had done, just so Everett could watch out for him. Again, Everett didn't seem very worried, but Quinton was a little taken by it.

At this point, I was so beside myself. I wasn't sure what I was doing or what I should do anymore. It seemed like things were just getting worse and I was lying to everyone. I was trying to make it work with Quinton. However, I was always preoccupied with what was happening behind the scenes and trying to keep both sides from going to war with each other.

Everett and Quinton both said that they were ready for a fight. I was so scared that someone was going to get shot though. I began drinking pretty heavy.

If I wasn't working, I was drinking from pretty much the time I awoke until I passed out. I would sneak between Quinton and Lincoln and felt bad and incomplete at both places though. With Quinton, he was always so upbeat and motivated. He was concerned about my drinking, and I could tell he judged me for it, but I didn't care.

I was severely troubled with the circumstances of my life. I felt like I couldn't open up to him. I had realized how much my life was about Lincoln, and besides my work, I had nothing left of the life I had been living.

I barely had a relationship with my family because I had been lying to them for the past so many years about what I was doing. As a result, I had to build something new. I was getting close with Pippa, though we had never really talked anything past a superficial level, and we started just chilling upstairs a lot and talking.

I got to know her and what's going on in her life. I couldn't help being somewhat jealous of her so uncomplicated life.

When I had seen Lincoln, it was usually depressing. I would sneak over there some nights. Everyone in the garage would be drinking beer, playing darts, and listening to music just like old times.

Lincoln kept playing songs for me. One song was called, *Angel* and another one was called, *My Girl.* I felt so bad for hurting him the way I had, but I didn't want to be there anymore. Going over to see him had only messed with my head and my heart, especially when Lincoln would dedicate these songs to me and tell me how he felt.

Also, Lincoln had went on to tell me how he couldn't live without me and he almost took his life. He told me that he couldn't stand me not being there with him like we use to be. He said the only thing that stopped him was that Chloe had come out to see why he was sitting in the driveway.

Lincoln really started trying everything to get me away from my family. He sent the cops to my home to do a welfare check on me. Quickly, he called me, and he was excited to tell me that he was sending the cops over, and I was supposed to say I was suicidal so they would take me away from my family and put me in our local mental care facility.

## Chapter 5. Strongholds Are Hard To Cut.

When they arrived, I pretended to be completely clueless and told the police I was fine. Then, I told Lincoln my family interfered and said they would keep an eye on me.

Besides that incident of him calling the cops to my home, Lincoln had also worked it out for me to get an apartment. However, I had made an excuse why that wouldn't work. He was constantly coming up with different ideas of things that I was supposed to do, but I would later tell him a reason why it didn't work.

In the meantime, Quinton and I were becoming more and more distant because he wanted to show me off, and I wouldn't let him. From everyone feuding, my drinking, and little freak outs, we were slowing fading away. What really started the beginning or end, was the night when Quinton and one of his buddies snuck over to Lincoln's house and were watching them in the garage when I was there.

As soon as I got back to my dad's home, Quinton said, "What are you doing?" I told him as much of the truth as I could without giving away that Lincoln and I had a relationship, and I was only over there to appease Lincoln so he wouldn't do anything stupid.

The whole situation made Quinton furious. I guess I made him look really stupid in front of his buddy.

According to Quinton, he had told his buddy everything that happened and how Lincoln was sneaking around the house. Then, they came up with the plan to spy on Lincoln to get some dirt on him by doing the same thing minus the guns.

Consequently, I could tell the feud was building because Quinton was talking about calling up a rough crowd that he knew who would come to take care of Lincoln.

At that same time, Lincoln kept talking about shooting Everett and Quinton. Afterwards, it wasn't long until the day came when I snapped at Quinton for no reason, other than I had been drinking all day and my nerves were shot.

After this happened, Quinton took off and we ended it. It was bittersweet. It was bitter because I had high hopes of being happy with him and sweet because I didn't have to juggle, sneak, and lie anymore.

In the days that followed, I saw Quinton a few more times when we worked together, and he still refused to back off from Lincoln. Finally, the day came when we were discussing it at work, and he wouldn't budge on stopping his guys from coming to rough up Lincoln.

In a last ditch effort, I acted like I had a tape recorder on the side of me that I was fumbling with, and then got up and walked out. I noticed his face before I completely left the room, and I knew I scared him enough that I didn't have anything to worry about anymore on his end. He ended up transferring to another house, and we haven't spoken to each other since that day.

As a result, I decided that I had to stop Lincoln from his feuding threats. Reluctantly, I went back to him. It was really hard. In one way, I loved him. In another way, I wasn't happy with him anymore and being away from him those couple months was sort of liberating. I could finally breathe when not around him. I wasn't constantly watched or controlled and told when, where and why. I wasn't afraid to mess up or come across that I was not perfect.

### Walked Into A Huge Bomb.

However, when I went back to Lincoln, I realized I made a bad decision, for I had walked into a huge explosive bomb. Somehow, Lincoln had gotten all my phone recorders for the last couple months and sat in the garage with a box of colored pencils and color coordinated every number. He was reviewing over twenty pages and hundreds of phone numbers.

Meanwhile, as I stood there, I watched him study the pages thoroughly, and he figured out some numbers and some were questions. Suddenly, he was furiously fuming with anger as he made me sit through a harassing interrogation process.

Out of anger, he frantically and hysterically demanded that I explain every single number while accusing me and degrading me by every malicious, nasty, horrible, and hateful condemning name that came to his mind. Besides that, sometimes he became semi-physically abusive by painfully pressuring my head as he pushed at my head with his forehead while calling me abusive names with spit flying out his mouth.

Then, he continued with his intimidation game to make me feel even more guilty and fearful by telling me all the good things he was going to do for his wife.

Furthermore, to make me feel that I was the bad guy, he continued to punish my emotions by telling me how he was going to make love to her. He described how perfect she was and rudely said I was garbage. Again, he spoke every other evil and horrible name he could think of to degrade me. By that time, I didn't care that I got busted for cheating. Again, I cared that I had nothing if I lost him, and yet on the other hand, I couldn't bare losing him at that moment.

I was utterly confused, hurt, and fearful at the same time. His abusive actions and words made me feel totally rejected and lost without him. With mixed emotions, I gave into feeling it was my fault. There I was again, bawling and begging him to forgive me and I believed I deserved everything that was said. I was hoping he would take me back.

When he refused me and told me he wanted nothing more to do with me, I got up to sadly go home wearing defeat all over my face. However, when he thought about me actually leaving and he saw that he couldn't control me again, he suddenly said something to make me stay.

In hindsight, that was only another trap to keep me a slave. Spiritual warfare is alive and striving. Lincoln was a prime example of a devil's advocate. If you don't know God's Word or how the devil operates, you will make yourself vulnerable to be attacked.

Later on, I learned that in the Bible, Jesus taught us how to discern between the devil's nature and his purpose, and the nature and purpose of Christ. In one scripture, Jesus defined the nature of the devil as a liar and the father of lies, and He referred to people who did not serve Jesus and were in darkness. He said it this way, *"You are of your father the devil, and it is your will to practice the desires [which are characteristic] of your father. He was a murderer from the beginning, and does not stand in the truth because there is no truth in him. When he lies, he speaks what is natural to him, for he is a liar and the father of lies and half-truths"* (John 8:44, AMP).

In another scripture, *"Jesus said to him, I am the [only] Way [to God] and the [real] Truth and the [real] Life; no one comes to the Father but through Me"* (John 14:6, AMP).

### Back With Lincoln Again.

Now, let me continue with my story. We ended up going camping for the weekend. It was the fourth of July. The whole family went and he would barely talk to me, but I was pretty silent myself. I couldn't believe my life. I had no clue what I was doing. I was feeling numb, so I drank beer, listened to the music, and went through the motions.

Then, one night while I was sitting next to the fire by myself and drinking, I was content. Everyone went to bed and Lincoln came and sat by me and reached over and grabbed my hand and pulled it to him. It was that gesture, which made me fall for him again. I needed that gesture to allow myself to feel loved and wanted again. It grounded me back into thinking I knew what I was doing with my life, however, I actually was strongly depended on Lincoln to tell me how to live.

Things became good again. Almost daily, we started going fishing or swimming. Again, we were always drinking beer. We would spend time with his friends, doing the same thing every night. Either we did pool, darts, or cards. Life was another party.

### Fits of Rage.

Let me stop for a moment to share how anger causes strife and division. The Bible says to not sin when angry, for it will give the devil a foothold to put bitter offense and unforgiveness in one's heart, which can lead to a sudden blowout attack of strife and division. The scripture says it this way, *"In your anger do not sin, Do not let the sun go down while you are still angry, and do not give the devil a foothold"* (Ephesians 4:26-27, NIV).

In other words, after being angry against another person and before you sleep that night, be quick to forgive and give the situation to the Lord, or else, the devil will use you to attack that person.

One night, while Layla and I were drinking and sitting in her house, she started to turn really snaky, which wasn't unusual for her. She started throwing side comments at me. When I arose to walk away from it, she ran behind me and clawed my face.

To get her to let go, I threw myself back into her, which knocked us both down, but she still had her nails gouged in my face. I tried getting her to let go by grabbing her hands, but then she tried punching. I grabbed her and screamed to let go; it snapped her out of her stupor and she ran upstairs.

Then, I went to see Lincoln and woke him. I told him I was leaving and explained why I had to leave. He was more concerned I didn't tell anybody what she did or call the cops because he didn't want her getting into trouble over it. Therefore, he came up with a cover-up story of what I need to tell my family and people we worked with, when they asked what happened because my face was awful looking. I seriously thought I would have huge scars because of it, and I was amazed that it healed so well within a few weeks.

Shortly after that, Layla ended up moving out of her parent's house and I never spoke to her again. I knew she viewed me as a threat to her family and she blamed me for what was happening because I was disposable. Her father will always be her father. Therefore, it made me an easy target for her to project anger. Sometimes, we would see each other but never talked to each other again.

### I Wondered What
### I Would Do With My Life.

As timed passed, I spent my eighteenth birthday deer hunting with Lincoln and a bunch of his buddies. We had a big keg party in the basement of his deceased parents' house in his hometown. We drank until the wee hours in the morning, and we were supposed to get up and go hunting but it was blizzard conditions. Since we were all hungover, we started drinking again and played cards.

After my birthday, I started thinking what I was going to do with my life. Lincoln always said he was going to marry me when he could, and I began to question if he was going to keep his word. I didn't pressure him for I wanted it to be completely on his accord.

My relationship with him continued, and we still spent a lot of time together. We did a lot of ice fishing. That year I ended up catching a twenty-five pound Northern on the small lake outside of our town. When it came to surface, it looked like a small alligator lying across the fish house floor. I ended up having it mounted.

Eventually, things began to change between Lincoln and me. Because I was eighteen years old, Lincoln's wife said there was no reason for me to stay there all the time and I silently agreed. It was awkward for me to be there, and Lincoln didn't understand when I wanted to go home. When Chloe started putting her foot down, it was kind of a relief for me.

Meanwhile, Lincoln and I hung out during the day doing our own thing, and usually went fishing together and drank beer, which I didn't mind because I loved to fish. Then, in the evening, we would part our own ways. He hated the idea of me going out and drinking with other people. He would discourage it to no end. However, I was liking my freedom, so I let it go in one ear and out the other.

### My Fling Was Short with Wyatt
### Due to Lincoln's Rage of Anger.

When spring time came around, I met one of my friend's cousins named Wyatt. He was short with long shoulder length brown hair and brown eyes. He usually wore black and leather because he rode a motorcycle and had carried himself like he was really something. He lived downtown in an apartment with two of his friends. They seemed like such an odd group of friends held together by partying and each

## Chapter 5. Strongholds Are Hard To Cut.

helping out with a portion of the rent.

I didn't really hide this fling from Lincoln. When I told him, he started crying and begged me to break it off with him. I didn't really give him an answer, but I already knew that I would. It was only a few days into seeing him, and I could tell he was such a womanizer. You could just tell he wanted something stable, but his lust for women overtook him. Thankfully I caught on early, but I would occasionally hang out with him whenever I was home drinking alone and bored.

One night, Wyatt planned a romantic camping trip for us two. It was outside of our town. I met him at his apartment and drank a few beers with him, but I decided I didn't want to go with him. Then I left to drink beer with Lincoln instead. A little while after I arrived, I realized that I didn't have my phone, and I left it at Wyatt's apartment. I told Lincoln I was going to get it, and he said he wanted to go with me, so he drove.

We came to Wyatt's place and his friends told me that he went to the campsite with this other girl and he had my phone with him, so I told Lincoln we had to go out there. When we arrived at the campsite, the girl he brought was sitting out by the fire, and he was in the tent. Lincoln sat in my jeep while I went to get my phone.

As I came walking up, Wyatt came out and met me the rest of the way. He tried explaining himself and his situation, but I told him I just wanted my phone. He insisted on explaining himself, and I kept telling him that I don't care and I just wanted my phone. He finally gave it to me, but then he didn't want me to leave. I walked away and got back in the jeep anyway.

He followed me and kept telling me to come talk to him, and I could tell Lincoln was angry, and he was getting ready to blow his fuse.

Then, Lincoln blew his stack as he started telling Wyatt to leave me alone. Wyatt stood in front of my jeep to prevent me from leaving and that was the wrong thing to do with Lincoln behind the wheel.

Consequently, Lincoln's jealousy turned into a violent rage against

Wyatt. Aggressively, Lincoln put the Jeep in drive and took off pushing Wyatt. He could have killed him, but Wyatt quickly jumped onto the hood of my jeep.

Then out of spite, Lincoln stomped heavily on the gas. I panicked and with a desperate voice, I yelled at Lincoln shouting, "Stop! You are going to hurt Wyatt!"

Despite how I tried to stop Lincoln, he determined to bully Wyatt by turning into a violent psycho mode, and he wouldn't listen to me. I had no idea how fast he was going, but then he turned the wheel sharp enough for Wyatt to fly off it.

That was the last time I heard from Wyatt, and I could definitely understand why. Being around Lincoln had almost cost his life.

### I Began To Fight Against Lincoln Stealing My Will.

After the above crazy incident, Lincoln would occasionally bring up Wyatt while throwing little jabs at me. However, it appeared that he was seeing that the little jabs were not affecting me anymore. It wasn't because I didn't love him either, because I loved him. The comments didn't bother me because I felt that he would never leave Chloe as he previously promised. I never brought it up either because I wanted him to be the one to do it.

Somehow, I felt being married to him would be the ultimate devotion to me, but I didn't believe that he would ever be devoted to me, so why should I devote myself to him?

Soon after that, one evening we were sitting outside the house, and we had been drinking all day and I wanted to leave. He had taken my keys so I couldn't drive and I was furious. He had never cared if I drove drunk any other time. He didn't want me wandering off and finding somewhere else to drink. He was throwing my cheating in my face, and I brought up the fact that he was still married and had been with her all these years, so I didn't want to hear it.

That time, Lincoln looked surprised at my remarks, but it still began escalating to the point where he was aggressively pushing his face into mine while talking very low and fierce with spitting as he talked.

Finally, I jumped up and demanded my keys. He wouldn't give them to me. So, I took off walking and made it half-way through the yard where there was the case of beer we just bought. I grabbed a can of beer, chucked it at his head, and then I grabbed another can chucking it again at his head. I continued one after another and as fast as I could. I hit him a couple times but mostly hit the aluminum screen door behind him.

Throwing the filled beer cans at him had really made Lincoln angry. He started yelling at me, *"Stop, Stop, Stop..."* At the same time, he was trying to cover-up and stop me because Chloe was in the house and would come out any minute to see what all the commotion was about. However, at that point, I didn't care anymore. I threw a couple more before I finally stopped.

Afterwards, I felt drained and extremely drunk, so I decided to stay. Lincoln didn't say too much more. I think he was incredibly surprised by my actions because I had never gotten physical with him, and he wasn't quite sure how to take it.

## I Blamed Myself.

One evening, I went out to drink with Bruno, a mutual friend of mine, and also a friend of Lincoln. I thought it was a completely platonic relationship, and I would be completely fine with him, but I was wrong. After drinking with Bruno throughout the evening, I went to leave, but he told me to sleep on his couch so I wouldn't get picked up for a D.W.I. driving through town. I reluctantly agreed.

Sometime during the night, Bruno sexually assaulted me. When it started happening, I was still drunk and disoriented and didn't know how to confront the situation.

Therefore, I checked out mentally and later learned this is a common survival tactic to get through assaults and called disassociation.

When Bruno finally left me alone and left the living room, I took a mad dash for the door. However, to get out to the back, I had to run through a dining room that I didn't know Bruno was laying there. He heard me and jumped up chasing me out of the house telling me to stop, but I didn't stop. I kept on and ran to my jeep.

Once I got in, Bruno was right there, apologizing over and over again. I think it messed up Bruno. He couldn't believe what he had just done. He apologized over and over, breaking down crying and saying he needed to quit drinking. I just sat there smoking a cigarette, listening to him ramble and trying to process it.

I left not knowing what to do. I questioned and blamed myself, and I wasn't sure how to face this situation.

However, as the days went on, I was becoming more and more distant. It was one of those "secrets-keep-you-sick" deals, I think. Due to keeping it secret, I bottled up the incident, and it was changing me.

A few days after the incident, Lincoln began to notice a change in me. Then on a day when we were outside drinking, he finally demanded to know what was wrong with me. I told Lincoln I thought that Bruno sexually assaulted me. He began freaking out and said, "See, this is why I don't want you going out and drinking with people. I warned you this would happen!"

Then, he demanded that I report it. I didn't want to do it and just wanted to handle it on my own. He told me if I didn't report it, he didn't want anything to do with me and I need to leave at that time.

After he said that, more than before, I didn't want to report it because I felt that Lincoln was using this horrible situation to his advantage. I was thinking that was the way he would get revenge on Bruno for a falling out they had a few years prior. However, it was just lately they began talking again.

For some reason, I couldn't bear losing Lincoln at that moment. I reluctantly agreed to report the sexual assault situation. He ended up driving me to the courthouse and found me an investigator to talk to her about it.

After that, Lincoln sat there while the investigator had me explain everything that had happened. She told me it would be hard to prove without a confession. Immediately, Lincoln devised a plan with her to call Bruno and ask him about it and he would record it. She also wanted my clothes from that night, and I had to go and get them and leave them with her.

That night, Lincoln called Bruno and asked him what he was thinking. The only thing Bruno said was, "I don't know…." His voice sounded sad and I felt bad for reporting it. Bruno was arrested a couple days later, and my whole family was in shock. I was so ashamed. I refused to talk about it. I started drinking heavier than before. I absolutely hated Lincoln because I knew he was gloating.

I felt that Lincoln manipulated that whole situation to get back at Bruno. I also thought that Lincoln never once considered how I felt. He didn't ask how I was doing. It was only about what he felt should be done. I couldn't stand being around him anymore. I drank with him but really kept to myself.

I had pretty much made up my mind to leave Lincoln after that. I just had to figure out a way to do it without him freaking out and going crazy.

### Co-dependency at Its Finest.

One day, we went out fishing, and then I went home afterwards. Soon after that, Lincoln called me and said that Chloe left. I was thinking, "Are you kidding me?" It wasn't because I was happy or in disbelief. I was thinking that for the last seven years, all I wanted was for him to keep his promise of telling me that one day we would be together, and now I didn't even want him. The irony completely baffled me.

I went over there and he was really beside himself. He said that he was mostly upset because of the time they spent in marriage together, and it was a shock she left. I felt I was cheated out of the ultimate act of devotion that he would actually live up to everything he said he would do when I got older. It felt like I was finally good enough.

I also felt stuck and was double minded. I really didn't want to be there with him, and yet, I really didn't want to leave him at a time like that. So, I tried to make something work with him. There I was again, trying to fix his victim mentality and problems and not thinking of doing what was best for me.

We would hang out like usual. On the days I didn't have to work, we would go fishing, drive around, and drink beer, or go shooting. Then we came home, made supper, and sat while watching television. On the days I would work, I would come home, and he usually had supper done and beer stocked up for us.

Let me stop my story for a moment, and remind you that Jesus is the only way to cut ties with the devil and his lies. He is the truth, the life, and the way to victory.

Much later, I found that when you know Jesus Christ as your Lord, He will change your heart and life, and restore your life with peace and joy that you never had before and give you self-esteem. Lasting self-esteem comes from Jesus alone, and then once you know what you are worth, you will never again settle for anything less. That is how we will have hope and fulfill our purpose in life with great peace and joy.

My story continues in the next chapter and you will read how my alcohol abuse takes a dark twist. You will read how I left Lincoln behind and fell into another trap of drug abuse.

# Chapter 6
## Too Much Will Make You Try To Escape From Reality.

*"Hope deferred makes the heart sick, But when desire is fulfilled, it is a tree of life"* (Proverbs 13:12, AMP).

There are many ways sexual abuse will affect victims. Depression, anxiety, post-traumatic stress disorder, physical injury to themselves, lack of trust, or need to control are just a few of the many effects. Also, victims of abuse will try to escape from reality by alcohol and drug abuse and keep taking it until they pass out. They have lost hope and feel like there is no way out, except to escape their problems.

I still did not know Jesus Christ as my Lord and Savior and did not have any hope of getting away from the pain of my past sexual abuse. I did not know that through Christ, I would be able to stop alcohol and drugs, and through Him, I would be able to stop the process of allowing Lincoln to hurt me.

Let me share with you the kind of agony, depression, and struggle I suffered using alcohol and drug abuse as an escape and cover-up of sexual abuse and pain.

### My Drinking Was Out of Control.

Whenever I was being victimized by Lincoln, I was made to believe it was love that hurt me. The whole situation that started at twelve years old, grew nothing but toxic misfortune in my life. The toxicity of the situation came creeping from outside ways. I tried many ways to escape my past pain from everything that had happened to me. I began drinking alcohol until I was out of control. I was drinking to the point of blackouts and puking just so I could drink some more by this method of "binge drinking."

As a result, I couldn't even stand or walk sometimes. There were times Lincoln would have to carry me to the toilet when I would be trying to make it to the bathroom, because I would be bouncing off the walls. I even fell into the shower one time. Lincoln would carry me to the bedroom and try to make love to me, but I would just pass out on him.

Lincoln wasn't the only one concerned about my drinking. My friend, Alana talked to my dad about it, and they confronted me about my alcoholism and asked me to go and get some help. I was stubborn and became belligerent about it and refused. Alana tried one other way by talking to my boss to see if they could give me a leave of absence so I could go to treatment and still have my job when I came back. Then, my boss talked to me about my alcoholism, and I pretended to be clueless concerning the reason why Alana would say something like that.

It wasn't long before I ended up getting a DWI. I was driving a friend to the city to pick up her boyfriend. We drank there, and on the way back, I was speeding and passed a state patrol, and I was pulled over. During the sobriety test, I passed everything except I blew a .001 over the legal limit.

The officer was actually really decent about that matter and said he would just book me and release me to a sober driver. My friend passed her breathalyzer, so she drove my jeep to get me.

This made Lincoln upset when I told him what happened, and of course he lectured me. I didn't want to hear it because he never said anything when we drank and drove together.

As a result, I was fined, lost my license and had some jail time hung over my head.

### Leaving Lincoln.

As much as I tried to make it work with Lincoln, I knew that eventually I would have to leave him. His actions proved it.

Let me stop my story for a moment and share some wisdom about leaving your sexual abuser. The way to freedom from that abuser and deception is to decide to leave him once and for all, and don't ever go back despite his threats or manipulation. Then, have nothing to do with him.

God loves you and never purposed for you to associate with an abuser or marry him. Once you leave the abuser, God will be there for you through the painful process of healing. This truth could have helped me to avoid much turmoil and destruction in my life, but at that time, I did not know how to leave Lincoln.

To continue with my story. one night, I was at my dad's house when he was up north hunting for the weekend. He asked me to be at home for my sister's sake.

While I was there, I invited my friend, Clyde, to come over and have some drinks with me. We were upstairs drinking, listening to music, and having a good time. Pippa had a couple friends at the house, and she was hanging out with them also.

Eventually, it was getting late, so I told Clyde he could stay the night if he wanted. We went downstairs to go to bed. A little while later, we were both almost asleep when I heard a man's voice say, "Don't move or I'll smoke you!"

I didn't move and was confused for a minute. Suddenly, it dawned on me that it was Lincoln. The room was pitch dark. Immediately, I jumped up and ran to turn on the light.

With the light on, I saw Lincoln pushing Clyde down in the bed with his arm cocked back, ready to punch him. I was surprised and shocked at that moment and I screamed, "Lincoln, what are you doing?"

As I looked at him, I clearly noticed the absurd and obnoxious look on his face. It was completely deranged and mean looking. His eyes seemed crazy and his face was completely contorted into something downright ugly as the appearance of a man who lost his mind.

## Chapter 6. Too Much Will Make You Try To Escape from Reality.

Slowly he looked at me, but when he saw that I was only wearing a bra and underwear, he started to whimper and walk towards me really helpless looking, trying to cover me up. He grabbed a little blanket and carried me out of the room and pushed me into the bathroom.

I sat down on the toilet and he sat on the floor in front of me and buried his head in my lap and just cried. I had never been so sick to my stomach knowing something was not right with him. I tried to think I would appease and console him by saying, "There, there," but I couldn't even fake it with sympathy.

After a minute or so, he sort of pulled himself together and his anger set in. He became meaner. Then, Lincoln told me he had crawled on top of the garage so he could watch me. I was really surprised. However, I wasn't doing anything with Clyde, so I didn't see what the big deal was about. When he saw me go to bed, he crawled in through the upstairs window.

Once Lincoln saw the aggression wasn't phasing me, he started to reason with me. He begged me to come home with him and I refused. I told him I would see him in the morning. He left with his shoulders wearing defeat all over them, and I started to feel sorry for him but knew the love was gone.

I went back to the bedroom to see if Clyde was alright. He was fine but completely baffled about what just happened. To appease him, I made up some lame excuse.

Then I went to talk to my sister and her friend because it was her bedroom upstairs. It was obvious that it scared Pippa seeing Lincoln coming through the window and running downstairs. I was wondering if she was alright and she said, "I'm ok!" I tried to make an excuse for Lincoln's behavior, but how do you really explain something like that? After that, I went back to bed.

That next morning, I made good on my word and went to talk to Lincoln. He was limping and I asked what happened. He began to tell me how his night got even more interesting after he left my dad's house. I guess he went home and went to bed for a little while. After he went to sleep, Jackson came running and told him to grab his gun because some guys followed him home from the bar.

Lincoln wasn't sure why this occurred, so he grabbed his shotgun and they ran outside and Jackson grabbed his gun from the trunk of his car. A truck whipped around the block and they all had a standoff until the police came around the corner. The truck started taking off and hit Lincoln throwing him into the curb. Then, they were all surrounded by the police with their guns drawn. They took the guys into custody from the truck, and Lincoln's son took off before the police got him, but they let Lincoln go. He never said much about coming into my dad's house. Therefore, I didn't bring it up.

That night, my dad came home from up North and my sister told him what Lincoln had done. My dad was livid and had enough of Lincoln always thinking he could waltz in his home, so he called the cops and reported it. Then my sister actually told me our dad called the cops and is pressing charges. All of those circumstances made me think on one question, "Could things get anymore twisted?"

Meanwhile, I left to give Lincoln a heads up. While I was at his house, the cops showed up to arrest him. He told me to contact one of his good friends for bail money. He was charged with a felony level breaking and entering. Then, he was released the next day.

When Lincoln got home, all I heard about was his violent death threats he was plotting to get back at my dad. In a furious, frustrated, and daring tone of voice, he shouted, "Your dad is a dead man, and I am going to sit back and shoot him while he was out hunting and make it look like an accident!" I didn't say much because I knew I was going to leave him.

It wasn't long after that when I left Lincoln. I didn't know how to tell him, so I wrote him a note while I was at work explaining that I needed time to be by myself because things were getting crazier and I needed a break.

After work, I went to his house, sat down and gave it to him.

## Chapter 6. Too Much Will Make You Try To Escape from Reality.

Immediately, he started crying and said he knew that was coming. He asked if I would spend one last night with him and I agreed. We sat up drinking, listening to music, talking, and crying, but I knew I had to be done.

When we went to bed, Lincoln just held me. The next morning Lincoln got up and went to work sometime really early, and I got up and packed what I could pack so I could be gone before he came home.

When I left I felt free, but I felt so unimaginably lost. I had no life really outside of Lincoln for everything revolved around him.

### Drinking To Forget!

After that, my drinking grew worse. I had started to see a guy named Bo, but he wasn't a winner by any means. He didn't work and he didn't have a car. Besides that, he lived with Clyde and that's how I met him. The relationship started a big feud between Bo and Clyde because Clyde had obviously liked me, but I didn't like Clyde in the same way he liked me. Clyde was fun to drink with but wasn't what I wanted to date. He seemed really clingy.

I was drawn to Bo because he was cocky and more outgoing, but the downfall was that he had nothing going for him. However, he knew how to party. Bo looked like a tough boxer and acted like he was on top of the world. He had brown eyes and his head was covered with wild crazy curls. He had that countrified and tough look to him.

Our rendezvous was shortly lived, but it was a life-changer. He came to stay with me at my dad's house, and we were together for a month and a half. I still worked, but he didn't have a job. So, he did whatever he wanted to do until I came home from work. Then, we hit the liquor store and drank the rest of the evening, often well into the morning while listening to music, playing cards, and doing whatever.

Some nights though, I would be depressed because I missed Lincoln, and I wasn't quite sure what I was doing in life anymore. I left the only life I had, and I had no clue what to do with myself. I would make some of my own choices before, but usually, Lincoln had so much say in the course of my life.

Therefore, on the nights I felt like this, I would usually sit at the computer by myself, listening to music. However, about once a week I would leave Bo at the house by himself, and I would meet up with Lincoln and drink with him.

After meeting up with him, it usually didn't take long to remind me why I left. He would sit there and criticize everything I had going on in my life. Besides that, he tried to convince me to come back to him. He would start kissing and rubbing on me. Then, I got disgusted and left again.

I was so lost in life and I was still drinking to the point of blackouts. About a month after Bo and I were together, he left me because I left him to go drink with Lincoln. I didn't come home until four o'clock in the early morning and he had already left. I didn't even bother to see where he had gone. I just passed out.

The next morning, one of my friend's named, Vivian, wanted me to give her a ride to the jail so she could visit her boyfriend. I told her I would. I was still drunk and we had a full liter of *Southern Comfort* to drink. While Vivian was in the jail visiting him, I sat in my jeep drinking the *Southern Comfort.*

My sister had called at one point and wanted a ride home, so I went to pick her up while waiting. Then, my sister, her friend, and I went back to the jail.

Shortly afterwards, Vivian came out and we headed home. My driving was horrible and Vivian started yelling at me to let her drive, but I refused and started to speed. I was flying down the side roads until I saw that it was my road to turn, but I was going too fast still. We hit the curb and flew into a tree. Vivian and I hit the windshield and my sister and her friend took out my center counsel.

I just started laughing and Vivian could not believe I was laughing and she started yelling at me. I threw my Jeep in reverse and drove down the block to my dad's house. Quickly, I went in and hid in the clothes dryer because I knew the cops would be coming soon and they did. My sister told them I had left with a friend and she didn't know who left with me. The cops told her to tell me to contact them because they needed to speak to me about the situation.

The next day, I woke up and didn't remember anything. I called Vivian because I knew I was with her last, and then she told me I crashed my Jeep. I didn't believe her, but she told me to go outside and look. I was completely bewildered because I had no recollection until hours later when fragments slowly came back to me. Bo came back later that afternoon and we made up.

Also, my dad came home from his hunting trip. When he heard what happened, he convinced me to go to the police station and turn myself in. My dad brought me there. The police ticketed me for leaving the scene of property damage, and the cop lectured me also.

The cop pretty much said he knew I was drinking. There was booze all over the steering wheel and beer cans under the seat. He commented that I better count my blessings for not being in more trouble than that.

I left relieved that I wasn't in more trouble than I should have been in when the cop ticketed me. I knew my license should have been revoked in the system, but all the computers were still saying it was active. If I was caught the day before, it would have been my second DWI in two months.

A week after that incident, I was given a court hearing located in the city where I got my DWI. Before leaving for court, I had to pick up Bo from his friend's house because he had been out all night. When I picked him up, he was acting really weird. Persistently, I kept asking him, "Bo, what is wrong you? What is wrong with you?" Finally, he admitted he was doing meth.

I was extremely upset with Bo because I was so against it. I had watched what that stuff did to those close to me. They had lost their minds from using it, but I did not have the energy to argue with him, so we went to my court hearing.

The court hearing was just a preliminary hearing, but I had to go see a probation officer after court, before I could leave.

When I was in the office, the probation officer asked if I had been drinking because they could smell alcohol on me. I denied it and when they went to go get a breathalyzer, I ran out of the building. We headed home and went straight to the liquor store.

### I Soon Replaced Alcohol for Meth.

When we arrived home, Bo, Vivian, and I started drinking some more. That night, when I was sitting upstairs with Vivian and Pippa, they pulled out some meth and started chopping up some lines. Instead of freaking out like I usually would have, I became curious. It was the first time I had actually been that close to meth. I had seen it before from a distance, but this time it was inches from my face.

My curiosity got the best of me and I did my first line. I waited for the effects to kick in and it took a little bit, but I slowly got sober until I completely lost my beer buzz. Pretty soon, I felt better than I had been in a long, long time. I had energy, motivation, and my mind felt so creative and I felt happy.

I went downstairs and I was there for less than five minutes and Bo could tell the difference in me and was asking what was up with me. Then it hit him and he straight out asked if I got high. I laughed and told him I did. Then we ended up going to get more.

Getting high became my new love. That's all I wanted to do and did it. I ended up running into an old friend named, Heath, who had just come out of jail, and I started hanging out with him. He would give me what he called, "Halves" and "Teeners," if I let him use my jeep. That was when I agreed and said, "Sure, here is the key." I wasn't really sure how much it was, but I knew we could get high off the bags for a couple days between Bo, Pippa, and I.

My life began to revolve around meth. It started to affect my work. I had worked at a job for over two years. Within just a couple weeks after using meth, I lost my job because I kept coming to work late. It

## Chapter 6. Too Much Will Make You Try To Escape from Reality.

was sad.

My bosses said they really didn't want to fire me because I was such a good worker. Furthermore, they said they were unionized and had to hold me accountable. I cried because it was another piece of my life crumbling, but I was also happy because that meant I could get high without limitations, and that is what I did.

I ended up ditching Bo one night so I could go out to get high. Bo left me for good and I don't blame him, but I didn't care. All I cared about was getting high. I still drank a little bit with it, but for the most part, meth replaced my alcoholism. I no longer felt that I had to have a drink to feel better. Due to drugs, I usually hung out with Heath and his girlfriend. They lived in a different town nearby.

Time passed and it was a little over a month after I started using meth when Heath and I were leaving my dad's house, and I noticed a car pulled out down the street right after we pulled off. Then, after it followed us for a good three miles, I said something to Heath, but he told me what I was experiencing was called paranoia. I knew I wasn't paranoid, though I was usually well aware of my surroundings, after living the last seven years with Lincoln's stalking me or as Lincoln called it, "investigating."

The car ended up following us for miles to Heath's house and parking a block down the road. For some reason, he thought it was a coincidence and brushed it off.

Then, we went in the house and walked downstairs where Heath's room was located and also a hangout room. I tried to play a game of pool with some of these people who were there, but I couldn't relax, so I told Heath I was going to go home and I would be back later. After I left and got on the main road, a county sheriff began to follow me. He followed behind me to the county line and turned around.

As soon as he wasn't behind me anymore, I called Heath and told him what happened. He seemed to think a little more about what was happening but just told me to go home and get some rest. I went home and chilled all day.

That night, I was getting ready to head back to Heath's place, and another friend named, Kamryn, called me to tell me if I was headed that way, I needed to be careful because the town was crawling with cops. Instantly, the unsettling feeling came back, but I was still going to leave.

Then about twenty minutes later, they called and told me Heath's house was being surrounded by cops. Promptly, I hung up and called Heath. I blurted out that Kamryn called and his house was surrounded by cops, but my phone died and before I could get to another phone, it was already too late.

The next day, I ended up going to see him in jail and he was talking really weird. He kept saying things like he trusted me and he'd never get me. I was really thrown off by it, but I told him I was going to see what I could do to get him out.

### I Was Too Naïve To Sell Drugs.

That night I went to another neighboring town to see his contact and let him know Heath was in jail. I was really nervous about going over there because I only had met him one time a few days prior, and I had heard some crazy stories about him. Not only that, but he was just a scary looking, heavier set dude. People called him Stetson.

Stetson greeted me surprisingly pleasant. He told me he was headed over to his other house, which actually was close to where I lived in the town over. He told me to come visit him there, so I headed over there. His house was completely furnished and had sliding doors with an outdoor deck and swimming pool that sat on beautiful landscape. The basement was where he hung out. It had a couch, a couple tables, and a stereo. It was actually pretty cozy.

We began talking and he asked a lot about me and I lied to him about most of it because I didn't want him prying in my life or discussing Lincoln. We talked for a couple hours and then I was going to leave. Before I left, he asked me if I wanted to get rid of some dope for him. He gave me three balls to start with and I said I would.

## Chapter 6. Too Much Will Make You Try To Escape from Reality.

I had no idea what to do with the dope, for I was so naïve to the drugs. I showed Pippa and she said she knew some people who would want some. I had no idea how to weigh the stuff out, so she had to show me how to do that, too.

It turned out that I actually got rid of it in the deadline he gave me. So, he gave me more, and it just continued like that. Stetson gave me three more balls and I would get rid of it. Then, we met back at his shed every couple days to exchange money and dope.

Stetson and I also began to spend more and more time together. Through the nights, we would meet up for the exchange, and then, we started hooking up. I knew he had a live-in-girlfriend at his other house, but he told me they had an open relationship. I didn't necessarily believe it, but what we had was working with me.

I didn't know how to let anyone into my closed life because I didn't know how to explain my past. In response, I ended up lying to Stetson about a lot of stuff I had going on in my personal life and I accepted this thing we had going. I felt bad, but I didn't know what else to say.

About a month later, Heath ended up getting bailed out by his mom and he was still talking weird, making the comments like, "Don't worry, I won't get you!" or "You're cool." So, I started to avoid him. I gave him the stuff that I held onto for him while he was in jail and quit talking to him for a couple weeks. Then, he slowly came back around.

When Heath came around, things became really complicated and confusing. At first, hanging out with Heath was fine. Then one day, Heath called me and asked me to pick him up and also his buddy to bring him to the store. I was very tired and I just wanted to go to bed, but I reluctantly agreed.

Once we came to the store, he asked me if I would run in and buy some muriatic acid because supposedly a person needed an I.D. to buy it. He gave me the excuse that he needed it to strip a floor for the basement where he was working. Again, I reluctantly agreed because

I was coming down hard and just wanted to go home to bed.

As I came back out and was pulling out of the parking lot, Heath supposedly remembered he needed something else. For this reason, he told me to drive across the street to the other store. When I parked, he asked me to get what else he wanted.

I freaked out though and told him to go get it. We sat and argued for quite a while before a cop randomly ended up pulling up to arrest me for an outstanding warrant I had for my DWI court case. Then, at the same time, Heath's friends pulled up to pick him up.

It was way too much for me to process at the time. I didn't fully understand until a couple years later that the supplies Heath was trying to have me buy were supplies used to manufacture meth.

I will never know for sure, but I really do believe Heath was trying to set me up with a manufacturing charge. However, the only thing that saved me that day was my stubborn refusal to go back into the store for him.

As a result of a warrant for my DWI court case, I went to jail for four days and because the jail was overcrowded, there were five women packed into a holding cell, sleeping on a cot mattress on the floor. I slept the entire time except the morning I had court. Then, I was released the following day.

### From One Kind of Hell With Sexual Abuse
### To Another Kind of Hell With Dope.

After I was released, I was several hours from home and did not have any money. I walked to a restaurant and tried using their pay phone to call someone to come pick me up. I got in contact with Heath, but he didn't have a vehicle and I was stuck.

Then some dude leaving that restaurant had noticed me. He was Native American and probably in his late twenties. He introduced himself as Abraham and told me I looked lost. I told him my situation, and he told me I could hang out with him until I figured out something.

## Chapter 6. Too Much Will Make You Try To Escape from Reality.

Having no way to get anywhere, I chose to hang with Abraham. It was the month of March, and the weather was still cold. So, he gave me one of the jackets that he wore and we took off walking.

We walked to get to a bus and checked out bus tickets, but there wasn't one heading North until the next day, so we kept walking. We headed to the liquor store and walked to his apartment. There was one other guy there, and we just sat and drank beer while I used the phone to reach someone.

Finally, I was able to contact Stetson, and he said he would get me. It turned out that I was close to one of his friends' houses, so I walked there. As soon as I arrived there, they got me high, and I just waited for Stetson to come get me. He didn't get there until much later that night, but I was content and feeling fine while he visited with his friends.

The car ride was unusually silent, and I wasn't sure what was wrong with him. When I asked him, he said, "It was nothing!" But as soon as we got back to town, he dropped me off at home and left.

My life started to get really weird after that. To try to explain something would only confuse people. Strange things started happening to me. The high started to change and I became super-paranoid. I tried getting sober and running back to Lincoln, but even he was different, so I started to avoid him, too.

My life went from living one kind of hell with Lincoln to another hell with dope. I loved being high because I didn't feel anything emotional anymore. I had a euphoria feeling from the drugs that I used as an escape from my problems and the real world.

One day, I went out shooting with one of my brother's friend, Grayson. Everything was going really cool until he drove me deep into these woods and started to demand me to get out of his truck. He was talking really crazy and I seriously thought he was going to shoot me. I thought Lincoln had something to do with it too.

Finally, I started talking to him just making up crazy things to get his attention away from whatever reason why he wanted to kill me. I persuaded him to stop shooting completely, and he sat back in the truck and listened to me occasionally while asking questions.

Following that, I kept feeding him more and more baloney with traces of the truth until he had to go back into town to check into what I was saying. I figured I could do damage control later. I was so relieved when I saw the highway.

After I got home, I felt that it was all over, but I questioned if that really just happened under the pretenses I perceived. Then the next night, I met back with Grayson and my brother at Grayson's house. He was working on my computer and he started talking about Bluetooth. I had no clue what that was. It seemed that he was talking to me in a third person dialogue and telling me in more of a subtle coerced tone that I wouldn't want certain things to end up on my computer.

Looking back, I feel like Greyson knew I was out there mentally, and he was just talking strange things to mess with my head because he knew it was getting to me. I wasn't exactly sure what he was referring to, but I knew he wasn't talking about anything good.

As a result, my body literally felt like it was being electrocuted. I couldn't breathe. I tried to shut off my computer before he could transfer something crazy into it, and I took off running. I ditched my shoes, my bra, and anything else that I felt could be a source for them to track me and I took off walking.

Then, I walked at least twelve miles to a truck stop and hitch hiked to another town an hour away. From there, I took off walking all day again. I had no idea how many miles I walked. My feet blistered so bad and I could barely walk at the end.

When it was about nine o'clock that night, the cops saw me walking and picked me up and called my dad to get me. I went home and slept for almost two days straight. Stetson stopped by to see me and he seemed a little concerned and a little angry at me about everything that happened the last couple days and he left. I had no clue what to think after all that.

## Unforeseen Paranoia, Anxiety And Depression from Meth.

After sleeping at my dad's house, I went off the deep end, which was from my addiction to meth. At that time, I didn't understand the dangers of using meth and how it affects your mind to make it crazy. Besides the drugs, my background with Lincoln didn't help. My background set me up for failure to begin with. Then, adding drugs in the mix had warped any kind of reality that I had left, which was pretty slim in that new life away from Lincoln.

I experienced the symptoms that people have when they are mentally ill. I began lashing out at people because I would perceive that they were out to get me. I was obsessed with satellites. I drilled my fillings out of my mouth because I thought it was some type of spyware. I rewired the fuse box. I was just doing some really bizarre things.

The most bizarre thing was when I was reading into these messages that I thought were everywhere for me. I would take just regular words and twist their meaning. I would read into license plates and think they were trying to tell me something. It was almost like I had to play this game and solve this mystery to get my life back.

My paranoia became terribly bad, and I couldn't stand to be around anyone. At that point, I quit using drugs and I locked myself in my bedroom and pretty much hid from everyone.

People would come around me, and it felt like I was going to shatter. I was afraid to move or breathe because I didn't know what was going to happen to me.

There were so many times a day I wondered if I was really living anymore because I did not recognize anything about my life and I had nothing to believe in.

I can't tell you how hard it was to not know what or who I was. I had lost complete touch with reality. However, I felt lonely. I missed who I was a year before the drugs. I even tried running back to Lincoln, but was too scared to stay. I literally had nothing and no one I could trust.

Depression and anxiety plagued me. I slept all day so I could be up at night when no one was really awake. I began cutting myself, which I never would have ever done because I just felt like I needed to release something to get all the bad out of me and let me see I was really living.

My life was like I was living a bad dream and I couldn't wake up. My mind had no reference point of truth. I lost color to my world. It wasn't until years later, after I had God in my life, I was walking outside and I saw color in nature and the realization hit me that I had missed seeing color for all those years. I was able to see them physically, but because of my mental state, I overlooked it and everything was gloom in my sight.

### Nowhere To Turn.

I would still see Stetson, usually once a month. I didn't really know what I was to him. I would be okay with our occasional meetings, and other times, I would freak out about being a booty call, but our routine stayed that way.

A year after I started using Meth, I discovered that Heath had set me up when he got out of jail. He had set up many of us, and we all received our papers at the same time. I was surprised, but I also wasn't surprised because of the weird comments he was making after he got arrested. That time I was charged with *Second Degree Sales of a Controlled Substance.*

Right after the first of the year, I tried working again. I was able to get a couple jobs from the job service program doing production work. However, each time I started working, I quit because my anxiety was so bad that I couldn't manage to do the work. My mind constantly raced, and I couldn't stop looking around me or over my shoulder. I couldn't feel right! I felt like I had lost touch with my reality and I had nobody to turn to that could understand me.

I tried reaching out in different ways to understand my reality, but it didn't help. I felt like I was ignored or people were lying to me. I couldn't take it anymore, so I attempted suicide. I contemplated it for a while. I was going to hang myself in the basement. I prepared the rope and everything, but I just couldn't do it. I kept thinking about who would find me.

So, I ended up slashing open my arms with a doctor's scalpel and taking whatever pills I could find. I woke up the next day in a pool of blood and a huge headache. I was disappointed that it didn't work. I hid my arms and I started to drink.

**Another Round of Drinks.**

After that, I started to drink more again. I continued to be paranoid and reading into things. I still hated to be around people, but when drinking I could find this oblivion where I didn't have to feel for the time I was in it. That was how I could manage to tolerate being out and about. I was a mess. Usually, I drank from the time I awoke to the time I passed out. It continued like that until summer began.

It was that summer when I put myself into an inpatient treatment place. I hated it at first. My anxiety and depression made it hard to sit through the groups. However, I started to mingle more and more with the residents. I still was really paranoid of everything, but I never talked about it. I usually suffered in silence.

I started to become accustom to living this way. I was able to function, but I read into things. I still didn't really understand reality. It's hard to explain, but I believed my life was happening even though I felt like it was some sort of an obstacle course to get my life back.

Because of that, I constantly would take ordinary things and investigate them for hidden meanings. For example, I would investigate things people would say, signs on the wall, and things that would happen. I always thought there was more to what things actually were.

Besides that, I had no idea what I was living for or what to believe in. I can't stress enough of all the ways I was completely messed up. I wasn't doing that well in treatment. I was doing the steps and the book work just fine, but when it came to putting it into practice to stay sober, I wasn't able to do that. I became high a couple times while I was in there and when I would come home on the weekends, I would drink.

After a couple months of being in treatment, I got a job as a hostess at a nearby restaurant. It was alright, but facing people increased my anxiety.

I was put on medication for my anxiety and depression. I don't think it really helped. I had a regular antidepressant, and then, I was put on another medication for anxiety and sleeping. The only thing that helped was my sleeping med.

### In Court, Jail Again & Probation.

I had court for my drug charge and I ended up taking a plea bargain. They hung twenty-one months over my head if I sat six months in county jail, and I was put on twenty years of probation. I was not looking forward to being locked up. Dread wasn't even the word for it.

I didn't know how I was going to be able to handle the confined feeling of doing time. I had done a little few days here and there and felt like I was going to lose my mind. I didn't know how I was going to manage four months.

I was still in treatment while working as a hostess, but I gave up trying, knowing in a couple months I had to turn myself in to do my time. Originally, I had put myself into treatment to avoid doing jail time, but since it didn't work, I started to self-sabotage what good I did have going.

As a result, I was kicked out of treatment a couple weeks later, because I had pierced my ears in my room and got a tattoo when I was told I couldn't go. Therefore, I went back to my dad's house to live.

Chapter 6. Too Much Will Make You Try To Escape from Reality.

# Falling Deeper Into
# The Rabbit Hole.

I had court for my drug charge and I ended up taking a plea bargain. They hung twenty-one months over my head if I sat six months in county jail, and I was put on twenty years of probation. I was not looking forward to being locked up.

I was only back in town a day or two when I had plans to go to the bar. I was going with a few friends who were in treatment with me. However, another person, Tobias who was in treatment with me, had called to see if I could find him some drugs. I ended up finding some, so Tobias had his friend drive to the bar to meet me and wait with me.

I had already been drinking for some time when they arrived, and we drank a pitcher of beer waiting for the drugs to arrive. I was starting to think the deal wasn't going to happen, but then my buddy, Thomas, called and said he was outside. I ran outside with the money and they gave me the dope in a cigarette pack.

I brought it back to Tobias and we went to the car to smoke, but when we got to the car, they said it was bunk. I tried getting my buddy to bring back the money and he said he would, but then called back and said the dude who he was with had taken off with it.

That made Tobias and his dude angry. They said that I had to get their money or the drugs back. I didn't even know where to start. We drove around for a while, but I couldn't find the car that they drove. I could hear them talking up front, and I heard one of them mention their gun. I was wondering what did I get myself into.

After a while, I asked if they were going to keep me until they had their money back, and they said they weren't letting go until they had something.

Therefore, I tried going to the house where the mom of Thomas lived. I went there to see if he went home, but he hadn't, and the mom hadn't seen him. I went down to Vivian's house, the lady I used to hang out with when drinking alcohol. She knew whose car they were in and where they lived. I asked if she would come with me, because I figured the guys who I was with might let me go if they didn't end up being at the house where we went.

When we pulled up to the house, the car was sitting there. As we were getting out, I asked Tobias if he had a gun because I wasn't sure if I had heard them correctly before when they were talking. He said, "Yeah." I started freaking out. I wasn't sure what was going to go down, and all I knew was that he was good friends with Stetson and Stetson could get ruthless. Stetson was once paid five-hundred dollars to cut a chunk out of some guy's nose, so I wasn't sure what these guys were capable of doing.

Because I had been drinking and was frantic to do what the guys wanted so they would let me go, I opened my door back up and pulled a little three-inch pocket knife out of my purse. The knife was petty, but I figured that having something was better than nothing to protect myself.

Then we went into one door and it ended up being the wrong apartment. The people in there said Thomas stayed next door. So, we went pounding on the door that was locked. I started to kick at it, but nothing was happening.

As I was at the front door, Tobias and his friend went to the window and were talking to Thomas's sister. They called me over there and I tried talking to her. She said he wasn't there, but I told her to let me in and she didn't want to, so the guys lifted me in through the window.

As soon as I got in there, I told her what was happening that Thomas ripped off these guys, and they were furious and wanted their money. By the time I got done telling her, Tobias and his friend were at the door wanting in. I even debated on opening the door, but anyhow I did it and they came in strong.

There was some guy laying in the bedroom sleeping, and Tobias went and grabbed him and started smacking him around. I started screaming at Tobias to stop and told him that wasn't Thomas and he

## Chapter 6. Too Much Will Make You Try To Escape from Reality.

stopped. I was able to get Thomas's sister to call Thomas.

However, Thomas answered and said he was going to figure out something. Then, Tobias said he wasn't leaving until he had his money or drugs.

At some point, Thomas's sister was going to call the cops, and I took the phone from her and told her not to call them, and we got Thomas back on the phone. We talked out that Tobias would take whatever was in the living room as collateral for his money and Thomas would meet them tomorrow to exchange money for the stuff back.

For this reason, Tobias and his friend started loading up the car with electronics. We ended up leaving and Tobias dropped us off by Stetson's house. I still had Thomas's sister phone and snapped it, and threw it in the yard where we were dropped off.

We called for a ride back out to the bar and went there to drink. After the bar closed, a group of us went back to Vivian's house to drink. While I was there, an officer called my phone wanting to talk to me about the incident that occurred earlier. I told him I wasn't willing to come to talk to him until after Christmas, just in case they were wanting to arrest me and then he hung up.

After that, I went on a drinking binge. I would drink to the wee hours in the morning until I blacked out. This is how I lived. Then I would wake up and start drinking again. It was rough. I was lost at that time. I didn't even recognize my life or know what I was doing. I was making one mistake after another, still reading into things for hidden meanings, and my drinking only made my depression worse.

Meanwhile, I made it through the holidays and was supposed to turn myself in jail during February. Right before I was supposed to go in, I took all my pills. I took over 7500 milligrams of Seroquel. My sister found me the next day and brought me to the emergency room, and I spent three days recovering in the hospital. I don't remember much, but I was hallucinating really bad.

When they were going to release me from the hospital, my dad had the cops waiting for me so I would have to get my time completed. While in jail, I was still messed up from all that Seroquel, and I think I was just running on empty of everything. I was there maybe a week or two before I was questioned about the incident that happened when Thomas ripped off those guys.

It turned out that I was being charged with two counts of burglary and one count aggravated robbery. I was shocked. I was the only one charged with the robbery because I had the pocket knife in my hand when everything was going on. I was so angry. I felt like I was just being railroaded.

I ended up taking a plea bargain for simple robbery for twenty-eight months in prison. Otherwise, I was offered two counts of burglary for thirty-four months and I wasn't willing to sit any more time than I had to, but I took a more severe charge.

While waiting to be sent to prison, my Dad came to visit me in jail. He told me my problems at that time were pretty much the result of my life with Lincoln.

I started to cry because I knew that he knew, but we very seldom talked about it. He told me I should report Lincoln for everything that happened while with him. I ended up talking to a detective a few days later, but she was real skeptical on being able to charge him with no evidence. However, she would open an investigation. It was later dismissed for lack of evidence.

## Prison Life.

The day I went to prison was emotional. The guards came to my cell bunk to wake me up at five o'clock in the morning to ship me out. I packed up my bed and the belongings I was able to take with me, and said goodbye to my friends. The guards came and got me and brought me to a bench where I was shackled around my ankles and wrists. From there, we took the elevator down to a cold garage where a county van was waiting for me.

## Chapter 6. Too Much Will Make You Try To Escape from Reality.

They were driving me to a State Prison. So many thoughts of regrets, disappointment, and loss crossed my mind. The only wish I had was to become myself again.

When I saw the prison, I was quite surprised. I had pictured in my mind a dreary building with bars on the windows and barbwire, but this prison was nothing like that. It was a campus that consisted of a variety of buildings all decently clustered around a courtyard with picnic tables and a place to walk.

There was also a softball field, a walk/run trail around the softball field, and an area where inmates could play flag football or cross country ski depending on the season. The most surprising part of prison was that it didn't have a fence around the prison.

The van pulled into a driveway on the side of the main building, where intakes and releases happen. It contained offices for different programs and people in authority like the warden or discipline office.

Also, inmates would go there for meals, medical appointments, med administration times, and school, such as G.E.D or college courses. They went there for Educational programs offering classes how to handle conflict, resiliency assets, parenting, writing workshops and more. The gym, church, and library were also in the main building.

When the van pulled into a garage, I was let out and brought into an intake area. I was asked a few initial questions to verify myself, and then I was brought into a holding cell where I had to strip down. I had to take off one piece of clothing item at a time and hand it over to a guards where they inspected it.

Then once I was completely naked, I had to lift up my arms, open my mouth, rub my hands through my hair, show behind my ears, turn around, show the bottom of my feet, wiggle my toes, then squat and cough three times. From there, I was able to get dressed in prison clothes. I wore a pair of unisex elastic waist khakis and a grey shirt made by the inmates themselves on a job site called, *Textiles*.

After I was dressed, I was brought to the property window where I received the rest of my state issued items that were required. Then I was brought to my unit.

I was stationed there along with all the other new inmates. That was the place we had to do two weeks of orientation classes where we learned all the rules, schedules, and ways of the prison. I think I was in culture shock for a while, but I adapted. I met some people and started working a job in another building.

It was maybe a month after I was working there and a really bad fight broke out. It was pretty bad because more and more women started in on the fight. There was blood and hair flying. The one woman who started the fight had hold of another woman the whole time while beating her relentlessly. The guards all came running in and sprayed the girls down with pepper spray. All of us non brawling inmates had to line up in the hallway where we were searched for any contraband before we were sent back to our units.

It was after that when I realized I was around another type of people who lived a way different lifestyle. It was strange because a majority of the women looked like everyday people, and most of the women I had met seemed like really nice people.

Shortly after that, I was moved to another place for treatment. If one has any drug related charge, it was almost mandatory he had to complete the treatment program offered, otherwise thirty more days was added to his release date. It was much quieter over there in the new unit, so I didn't mind. With my social anxiety and the way I still read into things, living in a smaller community was better for me.

We had groups all day. Our day started early, breakfast was at six forty-five in the morning. After that, we had gym that lasted for an hour. Then, we went back to our units for a three minute shower. Afterwards, we went to our rooms to get ready for the day, and there was an institution count.

When the count ended, we attended our group. After our group meeting, we went to lunch and came back for another small group or big group meeting, depending on the day of the week. Then we had count again. After count, we had to do chores. We had supper, and then, usually we had free time until we had another count.

The treatment was okay. I had a few complaints that I kept to myself on the general operations, but I thought it helped me some. I began to scratch the surface of my life with Lincoln and how it affected me.

I was twenty-one years old at that time, and the wrongness of the relationship was really starting to hit me. I couldn't understand why Lincoln would even want to love me at twelve, and there was panic that replaced the gullibility I lived in. I felt disgusted with myself and was scared that I was to blame because I let him do those things to me. I looked back on all those years where I thought I was having fun and in love, but I didn't know what to make of it anymore.

The knowledge I gained of my situation by growing up was a knowledge that can only be gained with age. It left me with a world of confusion and pain that I didn't know how to deal with. I talked about it with my counselor somewhat, but I didn't fully truthfully talk about it. I felt a lot of shame and guilt for letting it happen and allowing him to touch me, especially when I began to like it, which I didn't want her to know because I feared it made me just as guilty.

There was also the humiliation part of it all where I lived such a quiet secretive life. I felt so exposed by revealing any part of me. Because I didn't have a solid grasp on my reality, I later learned that the following devastating circumstances had made me completely clueless as to who I was. The circumstances included a combination of my past and how I had to live, and then compiling the situation with drugs and alcohol, and the experiences that came from a lifestyle devoted to that garbage.

It took a year to finish the treatment program. Then, I just stayed as a graduate for the few months that I had left. I met some women and started new friends that I still hold dear.

## Out of Prison!

When I got out, I felt determined to make a new life. I moved away from my hometown and started to work at two different fast food chains. I worked and tried to pay off my credit, fines, and debt. Things were going alright. I caught up with some of my family and made up for lost time. My mom and I started a new relationship. I had told her why I was so harsh with her when I was younger. I told her about Lincoln and that he sexually abused me. She was shocked and supportive of me.

## Started Alcohol & Drugs Again.

Afterwards, I was able to function and live a semi-normal life again, but I still had my unresolved issues and they still affected me. I still didn't have much of a self-esteem or self-worth. I was still a bit out of touch with my reality.

So, I started to drink just occasionally and that worked for a while, but then I began to drink more and more and pretty soon I was drinking and trying to party all the time again. I fell downhill fast.

The saying of addiction, "You pick up where you leave off," holds to be pretty true in my experience. It wasn't long before I was hanging out with old acquaintances and back into the drug scene. I ended up messing up both my jobs. I left one job and I was fired at the other one.

I was trying to dabble more into the drug scene and sell it to support my high, but nobody really wanted me to get back into it, because of how bad I got before. So, I was very unsuccessful at it!

## Made Friends With A Man Who Sold Dope.

Meanwhile, a guy named, Mateo, who also sold dope, needed a place to stay, so I let him stay with me for a while. It wasn't long before we became a couple. We were together for a couple months. There was a time when I felt like I just wanted to have a normal life and we quit using drugs, and I was trying to fake it mentally and emotionally until I would make it.

It only lasted like a week though, and we wanted to get high again. I ended up getting mad at Mateo a couple days later and kicked him out. He was arrested a day later on drug charges that he had out of the city. I visited him the next available visiting day, and he told me that he was just served papers by our county too. He was being charged with drug sales. Then, he proceeded to tell me that I was mentioned in the paperwork also. It was a bit uncomforting, but I didn't feel like I had anything to worry about because I wasn't really ever involved in his sales.

## Round Two.

However, a week later, I was detained at my apartment for questioning on Mateo's case. I told them I didn't know about his dealings and they said that's fine, and then arrested me for conspiracy to sell with Mateo. I literally thought it was a joke. I think it had me in a shocked state for a few days before the reality actually hit me.

It wasn't even a year later and I was back in jail. In the county jail, I spent eight months fighting my charges. I was offered several plea bargains, which I refused to take and took it to trial. The result was being found guilty and sentenced to sixty-eight months in prison.

Like my attorney told me, "If you lay with dogs with fleas, you'll get fleas!"

Before I share what happened after that, I want to take a second to explain how easy it is to get tangled up in legal troubles. I knew Mateo was a drug dealer when we got together. I knew he sold drugs while we were together. I just didn't typically know when, where, how much, or to whom.

However, because we were a couple, I was found to be just as guilty as Mateo and even had to sit more time than him because it was wasn't my first rodeo, and I had more felony points. I was in prison with people from all walks of life who were doing prison sentences for things that didn't always seem just.

One lady did a line of cocaine at a party over the weekend and then was struck by a car on Monday, which legally would have been the other person's fault. Because the drug still showed in her system when they both were brought to the hospital for serious injuries, she was charged with vehicular homicide when the person who struck her passed away, and the had to lady spend six years in prison.

Another gal dropped her cell phone while she was driving and was trying to grab it when she struck a vehicle. Unfortunately, the accident killed an infant child and she was sentenced for three years in prison for negligence.

Crimes are indirectly committed all the time. That is why it is so important to do the right thing and hang around people with good character! The Bible warns us about bad character. The Scripture reads, *"Do not be misled: bad company corrupts good character"* (1 Corinthians 15:33, NIV).

Read the final chapter to find how I got free once and for all from the consequences of the constant abuse in my life. I finally was able to live a happy life after all.

# CHAPTER 7
## God's Foundation Is A Firm Foundation.

*"But what does it say? "The word is near you, in your mouth and in your heart"—that is, the word [the message, the basis] of faith which we preach—because if you acknowledge and confess with your mouth that Jesus is Lord [recognizing His power, authority, and majesty as God], and believe in your heart that God raised Him from the dead, you will be saved. For with the heart a person believes [in Christ as Savior] resulting in his justification [that is, being made righteous—being freed of the guilt of sin and made acceptable to God]; and with the mouth he acknowledges and confesses [his faith openly], resulting in and confirming [his] salvation"* (Romans 10:8-10, AMP).

In this last chapter, I will share how to give your life to Jesus and totally break free from toxic relationships. Also, learn how you can have a positive motivation for the first time in your life, and learn how to not allow a sexual abuser to continue to victimize you.

You have a choice to learn how to stop failing in life and stop throwing your life away to drugs and alcohol. You can become successful in life and no longer allow your sex abuser to continue to victimize you by refusing to abuse yourself with alcohol and drugs.

**Back To Prison for The Last Time.**

Let me continue my story from the previous chapter. Once and for all, I found the key to be changed and totally transformed and live a successful life to please God. However, this did not happen until the last time I went to prison and when I became more desperate to find the key to freedom from sexual, alcohol and drug abuse and find purpose and meaning for my life.

Going back to prison was one of the most lost, broken, and helpless feelings I ever felt in my life. I felt so hurt that I felt numb. It was almost like déjà vu, except I had four years I had to sit. I couldn't fathom sitting four more years. I had no clue how I was going to handle it.

I started out again in orientation, just like everyone else. I met some gals in orientation that I still have friendships with today. One gal kept telling me to try out the faith-based program, but I didn't think it was for me. I wanted to just get a job and do my time.

Then, I decided to get a job taking a brush-up class that prepares inmates for college. It was something to do until I figured out what I should do with my time. The class covered almost every subject there was. I did so well that I ended up becoming the tutor for the class. I made fifty cents an hour, and a quarter of it was automatically taken for fines and restitution. I averaged about fifteen dollars every two weeks because it was just a part-time job in the afternoon.

## I Chose To Attend
## A Faith-Based Class.

Finally, I did something I didn't do before. I ended up going to the faith-based program after all. I figured I had nothing to lose and if I didn't like it, I could leave. Once I got to the unit, I liked it. I liked how the unit was set up and I liked the women that I was sharing it with.

There was one gal that was a couple years younger than me. She came up and greeted me so nicely when I got there. She was the sweetest woman there! She had really surrendered herself to the Lord. Her whole attitude was so positive. At first, I was skeptical and didn't understand her.

The classes were three hours in the morning. The program had three phases sectioned out in eighteen months. The first phase consisted of having lessons in character traits, boundaries, tactics and Bible readings.

Through the Bible Class, we started finding out where everyone was concerning their faith. When I stated about my faith, I shared that I grew up in church, but didn't ever have a relationship with God.

When I went to church, I had no idea about Jesus and His love for me.

I looked forward to hearing some good news in class. I sat listening to my counselor and some of the other gals were talking about God as though they actually knew Him. It threw me off but got my attention! Believing wasn't required to be a part of the class. The program was taught from Bible Principles.

From experience, I followed five major keys to have freedom from sexual, alcohol and drug abuse and toxic relationships. Let me share them below.

### Step #1. Key To My Freedom From Sexual Abuse, Alcohol, Drugs & Toxic Relationships.

It Was The first Time I Told the Truth & Shared All the Details of My Past.

*Free from Keeping Secrets &*
*The Torment of Guilt & Shame!*

Sharing our life stories was one of the various major assignments in our phase 1 faith class in prison. Before in other programs, I had shared a sugar-coated version of my life story, but I wasn't serious about it and I gave only enough to appease the requirement.

However, this time I was sincere and willing to tell the truth details because I had nothing to lose. I really felt like I was at my rock bottom and I was extremely tired of running and hiding my past. That is when I decided to lay out all my cards on the table.

I thought that sharing personal information was one of the scariest vulnerable things I could do. I made a life of hiding everything and finally, I was about to expose it all!

I worked on my life guide for a few days. It was just a guide we were recommended to make that we could use to guide us through the sharing process of telling our life stories. When it was finally my day to tell my life story, I was nervous but ready and looking forward to letting it all out.

I sat in front of my class of around twenty other women of all ages and races who I had really grown to know and built a relationship with them. I started out telling my story like I shared my story in this book. It was nerve racking at first. I stammered and stuttered, but then it was just like I fell into this trance where it just came pouring out. After four hours, I had shared my life in detail with those women.

In the past when I was in darkness and spiritually blinded, I had been ignorant concerning the devil's devices of torment. He made me feel tormented, which had once kept me miserable to living in doubt, fear, and worry by telling me that things were my fault.

Be aware of the trick of the devil. He will try to use the same stupid tactics that he used on me. He will lie to you and make you think it was your fault and keep you from forgiving others or forgiving yourself. Staying offended, bitter, and unforgiving are the tools the devil uses to keep you bound to your past mistakes.

The Bible says, *"Whenever you stand praying, if you have anything against anyone, forgive him [drop the issue, let it go], so that your Father who is in heaven will also forgive you your transgressions and wrongdoings [against Him and others]"* (Mark 11:25, AMP).

In my mind, the devil tried to make me think I was guilty and I was the blame. This kind of evil keeps the "what if's" and doubt churning. The perpetual self-doubt robbed my confidence, which kept me stuck because I didn't have the guts to become somebody. As long as you believe that lie, you can never be truly free from toxic relationships. Jesus is the only one who can change your heart and life, and He was the one who totally changed my life.

In continuation of my testimony, the raw secrets of the past were finally shared and I had nothing left to hide. When I was done, I literally felt drained. It felt like the war within myself was over.

Then, I had no idea if I was defeated or free, until I was met by the woman in my class, and she greeted me with such compassion. It was then when I realized I was free from all the torment in my mind, and I really believed I was a product of spiritual warfare. I felt much lighter the next couple of days, but I soon realized there was more work to be done. Telling the truth and getting honest about the past was only the first step at getting better.

## Step #2. Key To My Freedom From Sexual Abuse, Alcohol, Drugs & Toxic Relationships.
### I Understood That Sexual Abuse Was the Root to My Alcohol & Drug Abuse.

*Responsible To Make A Step
To Change My Behavior.*

I started seeing a therapist every week. We talked about the sexual abuse and I slowly begin to see that I was really a victim and not an accomplice. I was a twelve year old girl who was robbed of her childhood. I began to realize that I fell in love with the pervert because I was tricked into it and also because my heart was pure.

Although I did have faults of my addictions, lying, and manipulating throughout my teenage years following into my adult life, I became aware that the sexual abuse was the root.

After understanding that, I realized that even though I was a victim, I had the responsibility to change my part by changing my behavior.

That's what the faith-based program helped me to do. It taught me healthy living skills to apply to life so I wouldn't continue that vicious cycle of repeated offense and backsliding.

I learned that when I previously did alcohol and drugs, I was suffering in the pain of the past of allowing Lincoln to continue to hurt me.

Finally, my motivation to change my life was not letting Lincoln continue to victimize me by failing in life and throwing my life away using drugs and alcohol.

Also, I learned that by carrying the guilt and the shame of the past, I was carrying his baggage.

By understanding that, I realized I held the key to let me out of the internal prison I was locked in and become successful in life.

## Step #3. Key To My Freedom From Sexual Abuse, Alcohol, Drugs & Toxic Relationships.

*Desperate For A Life-Changing Encounter With Jesus.*

Soon after that, I found Jesus Christ and had experienced a life-changing encounter with Him. It was the most eye opening experience I ever had in my life. It completely transformed my life when I actually believed His Word without a doubt.

Jesus will completely transform your life, also. All you have to do is believe and receive it by faith in what the Bible says. I will share more on this later and show how you can actually believe without a doubt.

I was hungry for God to change me and it started during one of my one-on-one counseling sessions with my counselor. I told her how I daily sat in class hearing everyone talk about God and Jesus, as if they know Him and can feel Him. Then, I said that I didn't have that connection with Him and wanted to know Him. That is when she gave me an assignment to seek God.

When I began seeking Him, I flipped through my Bible reading scriptures where God said He was loving, merciful, forgiving, and our Creator who made us and so many other scriptures.

At first, it was frustrating because it was seemed like the same old song and dance I witnessed in class, but there was nothing that actually connected me to God as yet. I didn't realize it then, but didn't understand until later that the more testimonies I heard in class, and the more I read the scriptures in the Bible, the more frustrated I became because the Holy Spirit was stirring my heart with hunger for Him.

When you get tired of failing in life and you want to succeed, you become hungry for God to make Himself real in your life.

I like facts and evidence, so it was hard for me to have faith in God. I ended up leaving the assignment alone until a few days before my assignment was due. Then, while sitting in my room and looking out my window, I was looking at the trees, the grass, and the sky and it reminded me of a movie I once saw in jail called, *How Great Is Our God.*

Suddenly, God revealed Himself to me. I will never forget the feeling of knowing in an instant that I was important to Him. Without a doubt, I could feel embraced in God's arms and see Him everywhere I looked. God is Life and the Creator of the sun, the sky, the grass, and trees! He is the Creator of color, the sound of nature, and the course of nature! He created us and is within us when we give our hearts to Jesus!

What He did for me, Jesus will do it for you. Jesus is the same yesterday and forever and He will not change. *"Jesus Christ the same yesterday, and to day, and for ever"* (Hebrews 13:8, KJV).

Therefore, when we receive Jesus in our hearts, we will no longer represent the devil and His nature, but we represent Jesus to act like Him, talk like Him, and do what He did while on earth! The undeniably God became real to me and I felt so loved by Him.

The road to healing took a turn for the better for me. It may sound so cliché, but when God became a part of my entire life, my perspective on life changed. It was still work, but I had hope and I had someone to walk with me through every step of the way.

One day, I was sitting in my counseling session with my counsellor, and she said something so impactful to me. I had been sitting there reciting more in depth of what I went through with Lincoln. She looked at me so earnestly with the kindest blue eyes and pleaded, "Let your tears be your booze, Amy."

Those words hit me like a freight train, and I finally realized that healing from all the pain caused in my life was going to keep me from wasting away on drugs and alcohol.

So, for the remainder of my time, I took therapy and classes of all sorts, just to gain knowledge, healing, and empowerment. I took college courses.

One of the hardest parts for me was to get over all the anger. Little did I realize it then, but later understood that when you fall in love with Jesus and His Word in the Bible, you will hate evil and love righteousness. It seemed like the more I was able to sort things out, from what was truth and what was false, the angrier I became with everything I went through that was so unnecessary.

After that, I began to cast on the Lord the anxieties, worries, and concerns of my anger and past hurt. In the Bible, God says it over and over again that He will take care of you, so I gave Him my cares to let the Lord take care of them.

The Bible says it this way, *"Therefore humble yourselves under the mighty hand of God [set aside self-righteous pride], so that He may exalt you [to a place of honor in His service] at the appropriate time, casting all your cares [all your anxieties, all your worries, and all your concerns, once and for all] on Him, for He cares about you [with deepest affection, and watches over you very carefully]"* (I Peter 5:6-7, AMP).

It is not necessary for spiritually blind people to keep destroying their lives. If they only knew the truth that staying in abuse for years is unnecessary. The lost don't yet know that they don't have to keep abusing themselves by sexual abuse, alcohol, and drugs. They don't know that Jesus is the answer and the way to become free.

The Bible says it this way, *"But if our gospel be hid, it is hid to them that are lost: In whom the god of this world hath blinded the minds of them which believe not, lest the light of the glorious gospel of Christ, who is the image of God, should shine unto them"* (2 Corinthians 4:3-4, KJV).

Because the lost have not heard and cannot believe until they hear the gospel, that is why we need to share the good news of Jesus Christ to those lost and without Christ. If you don't tell them, then they won't believe unless they heard the good news that Jesus loves them and has a great plan for their lives. *"But how will people call on Him in whom they have not believed? And how will they believe in Him of whom they have not heard? And how will they hear without a preacher (messenger)?"* (Romans 10:14, AMP).

This is why believers need to share the good news with the lost in their daily lives, and also share their testimony of the good things Jesus did for them. When they hear your testimony of what Jesus did for you and how He transformed your heart, the Spirit of God will manifest God's love to them. When they feel His love, they will know that He is real and really loves them, and they will want to give their life to Him.

That is the reason why I wrote this book of my testimony and freedom from forms of abuse and toxic relationships.

In a nutshell, we are all here on earth and daily we are faced with good and evil. Things that are secular, not Heavenly, are from Satan himself. Therefore, a person's deceit, misdeeds, disobediences, addictions, and rebellion will actually glorify Satan.

The Bible says it this way, *"Now the practices of the sinful nature are clearly evident: they are sexual immorality, impurity, sensuality (total irresponsibility, lack of self-control), idolatry, sorcery, hostility, strife, jealousy, fits of anger, disputes, dissensions, factions [that promote heresies], envy, drunkenness, riotous behavior, and other things like these. I warn you beforehand, just as I did previously, that those who practice such things will not inherit the kingdom of God"* (Galatians 5:19-21, AMP).

However, things that are pure, honest, good, and obedient are part of the fruit that glorify God. *"But the fruit of the Spirit is love, joy, peace, longsuffering, gentleness, goodness, faith,* (Galatians 5:22, KJV). Also, we read this in another scripture that says, *"For the fruit of the Spirit is in all goodness and righteousness and truth"* (Ephesians 5:9, KJV).

You have a "choice" to do right or wrong. Your choice is an act of your "freewill." One day, God will hold everyone personally accountable for the choices they made in life. Whatever you sow, you will reap.

If you sow seeds of corn in a field, you will reap a harvest of corn. In like manner, when you repent of your sin and accept Jesus in your heart, you will be changed, and one day live eternally in Heaven after you die.

On the contrary, if you sow to do evil and love evil, and if you do not repent, the Bible says you will go to an eternal hell when you die. Now is the time to get your heart right with God. Jesus loves you and has a great plan for your life.

Some people's freewill choices can affect our personal lives in very detrimental ways. For example, when Lincoln decided to pursue me sexually, that was not my freewill choice, but I still experienced the damage of his choice and that's what I couldn't understand.

### Step #4. Key To My Freedom From Sexual Abuse, Alcohol, Drugs & Toxic Relationships.

*With Stubborn Faith, Refuse to Look Back.*
*Look Forward & Go Forward To Do*
*The Good Things You Never Did Before.*

After you let Jesus in your heart, you are a new creature in Christ and your old lifestyle of the past is all gone and erased by the blood of Jesus, and you are a new person in Christ. All things become new for you have become new. This means you don't think, talk and act like the world anymore. You don't act like you did before you were saved. Being a *new creature in Christ* means that you change to think the way Jesus thinks, talks, and acts.

To do this, start to read the Bible of God's promises, forgive those who hurt you in the past, and let go of your past. This includes letting go of the anger and blaming yourself or others. In other words, you must stop looking back and start looking forward to the good things God has in store for you. Believe and receive His promises as you act on them.

That is what I needed to do and I urgently needed to know how to let go of my past and begin to look forward to the good things of God. However, for a season when I was ignorant about thinking of my past, I was able to process that I was an innocent naive little girl who was tricked and manipulated into loving a man, and it created hell in my life.

For a time, I was focused on the past. It made me angry to think about Lincoln and the wrong he did. I had thoughts such as, "Why should he have his 'freedom on earth to do what he wanted,' (I say it like this, because, is he really free?) while I reaped the consequences of his choices of abusing me when I was young and ignorant and did not choose it?"

As I stated many times in this book, his abuse for so many years had led me down to Hell's road of alcohol and drug abuse with toxic people. That was painful to think about it, and was why I was angry thinking how it eventually led me to imprisonment for x amount of years, correcting the mistakes of my life and my character. It just didn't seem fair and the anger burned in me.

However, because I wanted help to be totally free from all the hurt and anger, I chose to do something I did not do before. By reading the Bible, going to Bible study, and partaking in groups, I learned how spiritual warfare works, and the injustice of it is part of Satan's scheme. I began to understand that it was the devil who used injustice to knock me off course trapping me in a pit of anger, hurt, and negativity.

Then, I began to learn about the power of God's promises in the Bible. They were PROMISES. Wow, I liked His promises and that He would never fail me or leave me, but always be my side as my closest friend who I could depend on in all situations of life!

I was excited about God's promises that gave me life and victory! Through the Holy Spirit, He would be my helper, my guide, my strength, my peace, my intercessor, my mediator, my attorney, my provider, my comforter, my miracle worker, my healer, my restorer, and everything I needed that man could never do for me. I loved His promises for He will always do what He promised. How happy I became to know that He is not a liar and will never change His Word. That was exciting, life-changing, and good news for me, and still is exciting and life-changing to me today!

God's promises say that He will restore us as we just trust Him. That right there was my anchor in the storm, holding me onto hope until I was able to get a vision for my life. I wasn't sure how or when or with what I would be restored, but I had faith that God would keep His promise!

Therefore, that was when I finally stopped looking back and began looking forward. I began doing what I did not do before. I was figuring out what I wanted with my life. I journaled, I collaged, and I prayed, which took all this process to map out a life I wanted to live. By being aware of spiritual warfare, I was able to move confidently in my own decisions that I will do what's righteous to honor God and live a life happily ever after.

I held tight to the saying, "If you don't know what you stand for, you will fall for anything." It is so incredibly true. I was also aware that life will still have its mountains and valleys, but the beauty of that is if you did not know sadness, you wouldn't be able to appreciate happiness. God is your restorer and will turn your past sorrows into joy that you never had before, and that's what happened to me.

### Step #5. Key To My Freedom From Sexual Abuse, Alcohol, Drugs & Toxic Relationships.

*Give The Devil No Room*
*To Defeat You Anymore.*

Jesus transformed my heart and turned my sorrow into joy as I learned to stand on God's promises and trust Him with stubborn faith. My whole family have always said I was stubborn, and finally I used it for something positive.

Through stubborn faith, I refused to allow my past torment anymore. I refused to allow the devil to win. Here is what the Bible says about submitting to God's Word, resisting the guilt, shame, torment, and lies of the devil. Then, the devil will flee from you!

The Scriptures say, *"But He gives us more and more grace [through the power of the Holy Spirit to defy sin and live an obedient life that reflects both our faith and our gratitude for our salvation]. Therefore, it says, "God is opposed to the proud and haughty, but [continually] gives [the gift of] grace to the humble [who turn away from self-righteousness]." So submit to [the authority of] God. Resist the devil [stand firm against him] and he will flee from you. Come close to God [with a contrite heart] and He will come close to you"* (James 4:6-8, AMP).

When I gave Jesus my heart and life, I became a new creature in Christ. *"Therefore if any man be in Christ, he is a new creature: old things are passed away; behold, all things are become new"* (II Corinthians 5:17, KJV).

The Bible says that in Christ, our past is gone, and we become more than conquerors through Jesus Christ who loved us. This means, I am a winner through Christ and never a loser. Jesus turned my heart and life around because greater is He in me than the devil in the world. From there on, I gave no room for the devil to defeat me.

Once you realize that Jesus gave you power over all the power of the devil, the power is yours and also belongs to every believer. In the Bible Jesus said, *"Behold, I give unto you power ... over all the power of the enemy: and nothing shall by any means hurt you"* (Luke 10:19, KJV). God's Word gives us confidence that builds our self-esteem and trust in Him, and we won't feel powerless, helpless or defeated anymore.

The Word of God gives us strength in knowing our victory in Christ. We need to take the promises of God and declare them in our lives and stand on them with confidence. *"For all the promises of God in him are yea, and in him Amen, unto the glory of God by us"* (2 Corinthians 1:20, KJV).

After four and a half years, I was released from prison as a changed person, and I will say I didn't ever feel the need I had to prove I was changed, because the way I lived my life was my greatest testimony.

I started working at an auto dealership in the detail department. It wasn't bad work. A month into working there, a guy arrived from down south. He was looking for work and was hired. His name was Zac. He was different. His voice and laugh were so unique that I couldn't help but smile. His eyes were a gorgeous ice blue and it was hard to unlock from looking into them, almost in an embarrassing way. He was so funny too and was always cracking jokes.

Zac's demeanor was so mild and gentle that it was almost too good to be true. I could just tell he didn't have a mean bone in his body. It didn't take long before we were dating. I opened up to him about everything in my life and he was so nonjudgmental. I genuinely loved him and it scared me.

The beginning of our relationship was like a whirlwind. We worked, then hung out every night after work. We would go swimming, spend time at each other's house, play games, and watch movies. I had never experienced something so real and open in my life.

Since then, we were married and created a family. We have a simple and content lifestyle. I work as a hairstylist and make an honest living and try to be an encouraging light in other's lives.

We are plugged into a phenomenal church with such caring and loving people. They offer an abundance of opportunities where we can take part and enjoy. The message is always encouraging and positive, so much so, it makes me want to go out and practice the message. I couldn't be more pleased!

To conclude this book, I want to remind you that it wasn't until I became a Christian when Jesus restored my broken heart from all the past hurt and devastation. He gave me an inner fulfilment, peace, and joy that no man or woman could ever give me. Only Jesus can satisfy you, give you freedom in Him that you never had before. Only Jesus can change your heart, passions, and life, and give you purpose to succeed in life.

For the first time in my life I felt loved, accepted, needed, and appreciated by Jesus Christ. It was His love that I experienced, which changed my life. Since then, as a parent, I strongly believe in meeting the basics needs of my children to feel loved, needed, accepted, and appreciated and show them God's love to build their self-esteem. Then, they won't try to find it in the world and get into rebellion against God and man.

If an adult or peer in the world tells your young daughter that he loves her and if she doesn't have self-esteem, then your child will be gullible to trust that person and let that adult take advantage of her. As a result, it can lead to devastation, fear, and mistrust because your child sought for love in the wrong direction and just wanted to feel loved, needed, accepted, and appreciated by their friend (s) in the world.

Besides telling your children you love them, there are many ways to show them the love of God as you teach them God's love and His Word by example as a godly and honest parent. The Bible says, *"Train up a child in the way he should go: and when he is old, he will not depart from it"* (Proverbs 22:6, KJV).

Because of the lack of self-esteem, many children and youth get hooked in sexual abuse, and smoking, and drug and alcohol addictions. They are looking for love in the wrong direction and have no hope or purpose to succeed in life.

After I accepted Jesus in my heart, He totally transformed me and I have never been the same. He gave me self-esteem and confidence that I needed to fulfill my purpose in life.

I found that only Jesus can satisfy your soul, change your heart and life and make you whole. He will give peace you never had before along with love and joy and Heaven too. He loves you and has a great plan for your life. Being delivered and staying free from toxic relationships begins when you give your heart to Jesus and make Him the Lord of your whole life.

Jesus loves you and has a great plan for your life. Let me share with you three scripture from the Bible.

The first scripture says, *"For all have sinned, and come short of the glory of God"* (Romans 3:23, KJV).

The second scripture says, *"For the wages of sin is death; but the gift of God is eternal life through Jesus Christ our Lord"* (Romans 6:23, KJV).

The third scripture reads, *"For whosoever shall call upon the name of the Lord shall be saved"* (Romans 10:13, KJV). You're a "whosoever" and this means it refers to you and all of us.

If you died today and you are not sure that you would go to Heaven, I invite you to say this prayer out loud with your heart and lips. *"Dear Lord Jesus, come into my heart. Forgive me of my sin. Wash me and cleanse me. Set me free, Jesus. Thank You that You died for me. I believe that You are risen from the dead and that you're coming back again for me. Fill me with the Holy Spirit. Give me a passion for the lost, a hunger for the things of God and a holy boldness to preach the gospel of Jesus Christ. I'm saved; I'm born again, I'm forgiven and I'm on my way to Heaven because I have Jesus in my heart."*

Once you prayed the above prayer and really meant it with all your heart, as a believer of the gospel of Jesus Christ I tell you today that all of your sins are forgiven!

As you show God that you meant what you prayed when you repented of sin, you will let go of the old lifestyle and God will deliver you out of all your problems.

I love this scripture that reads, *"When the righteous cry [for help], the Lord hears And rescues them from all their distress and troubles"* (Psalm 34:17, AMP). God will deliver you out of the hands of the wicked when you really mean it to live for Jesus and not go back into darkness anymore.

Commit your all to Jesus, and read and believe the Bible. Also, attend a full gospel church where you can fellowship with a new family of godly men and women and be taught to enjoy the things that God has in store for you. Go where they teach you how to live in victory and win souls to Jesus Christ.

Jesus loves you and has a great plan for your life. It is never God's plan for you to be connected to a toxic abuser who steals your freewill. All things are possible with God in agreement with the promises of God! All things are possible for you as you believe and take a step of faith to act on His promises. The Bible says, *"For with God nothing shall be impossible"* (Luke 1:37, KJV).

Never forget that you can be confident and trust in the Lord, for God is good and does not bring you into abuse, shame, bondage, fear and devastation. Therefore, disconnect from all abuse and toxic people, and never go back into the past lifestyle. Go forward and God will do miracles for you and He will bring you into His purpose and plan for your life.

Always remember that you are more than a conqueror in Christ Jesus, for greater is He in you than the devil in the world, and always remember to run to God and not from God because He loves you and has a great plan for your life!

# About the Author

Amy L. Smith enjoys her career as a hair stylist and also loves to fish and camp with her husband and children. She is the wife of Zac Smith and mother of two sweet and adorable daughters.

Amy has a love for Jesus Christ and has a special compassion to help children, teens, and adults become free from abuse. When she shares her testimony, she tells how she experienced sexual abuse and was manipulated to keep it a secret for eight years, and shares about her suffering from alcohol and drug abuse. After she became totally free, she wrote her book to share her life story and show people the key to freedom from abuse, victim mentality, and toxic relationships.

She enjoys giving people hope and encouraging them by sharing her personal testimony of overcoming sexual, alcohol, and drug abuse through Jesus Christ who totally transformed her heart and life. Also, she shares how God gave her a Christian husband, Zac Smith who genuinely loves her. Amy carries a powerful message to help people get free from any kind of abuse.

Made in the USA
Monee, IL
11 March 2020